Global Doodle Gems Volume 15
"The Ultimate International Coloring Book...an epic Collection from Artists around the World!"

Leen Margot colored by Laety Esperanza

Nicole Whelan

Laurie Beauchamp

Fafahe colored by Solveig Fille Odin

Casey Gilmore colored by Laurence Roucou

Heather Richards colored by Laurence Roucou

Cathy M.

Neeti Goswami

Iben Lykke Højholdt

Lynniex Doodles colored by Zenfeerie

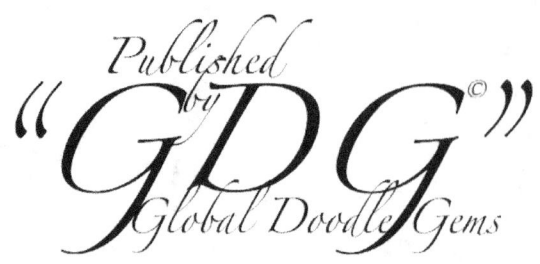

Share your colored versions with us! We love seeing your results and hearing from you we are social!

The Official FB book page, stay on top of what we have in the works!
www.facebook.com/globaldoodlegems
The Community group, share your colored pages, meet the artists, enjoy exclusive freebies, take part in community Charity books and so much more......
www.facebook.com/groups/globaldoodlegems/
Follow us on Twitter.... @GlobalDoodlegem
We are on Instagram too
@globaldoodlegems for instagram
...and if you are not social like that we have a blog
globaldoodlegems.wordpress.com

Copyright © 2016 Global Doodle Gems
All rights are reserved by Global Doodle Gems.
Duplication of pages for personal use are allowed. You are invited to color the pages then scan/post your coloured versions to social networks, mentioning the book title and author/artist (Global Doodle Gems).
All artwork and images are protected by copyright laws. This book or any portion thereof may not, otherwise, be reproduced and/or distributed or transmitted without the express written permission of the artist/publisher of Global Doodle Gems.
All of us from the Global Doodle Gems wish you a colortastic time and look forward to seeing your wonderful color results online!

Contributing Artists

1. Lynniex Doodles
2. Laurie Beauchamp
3. Heather Richards
4. Nicole Whelan
5. Cathy M.
6. Leen Margot
7. Casey Gilmore
8. Fafahé
9. Iben Lykke Højholdt
10. Neeti Goswami

Chapter 1
Lynniex Doodles
England

Facebook : Lynniex Doodles

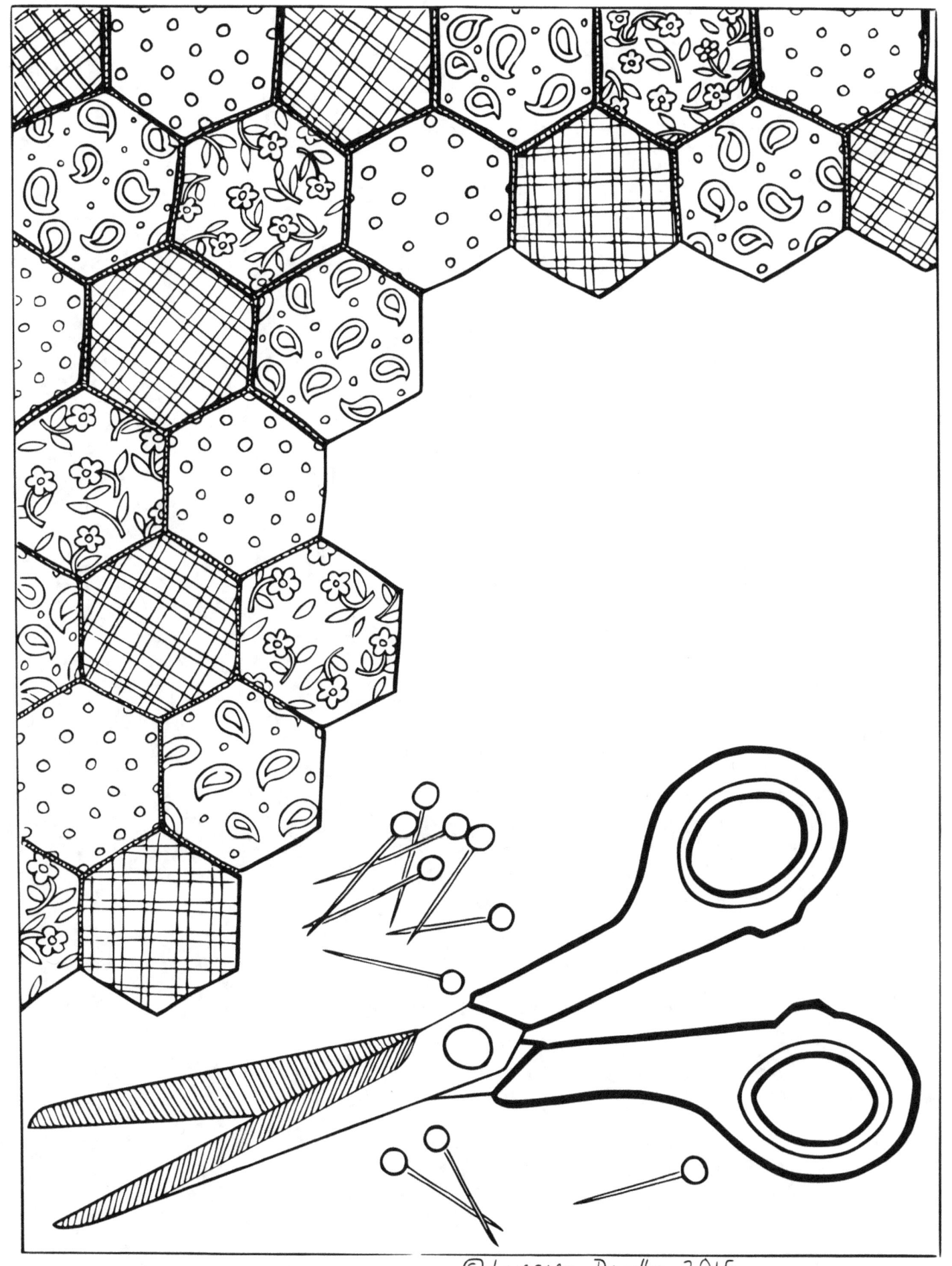
©Lynniex Doodles 2015

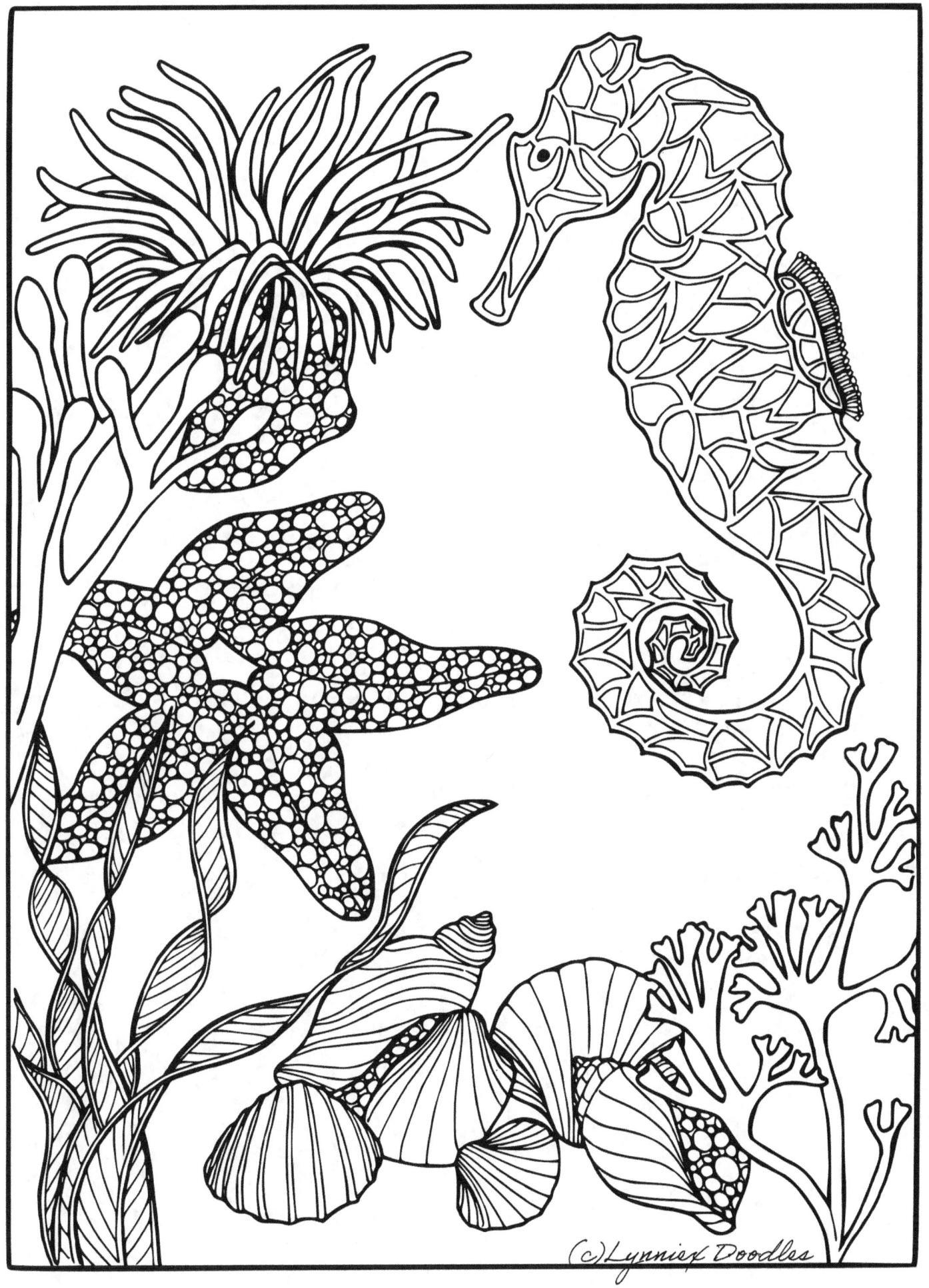

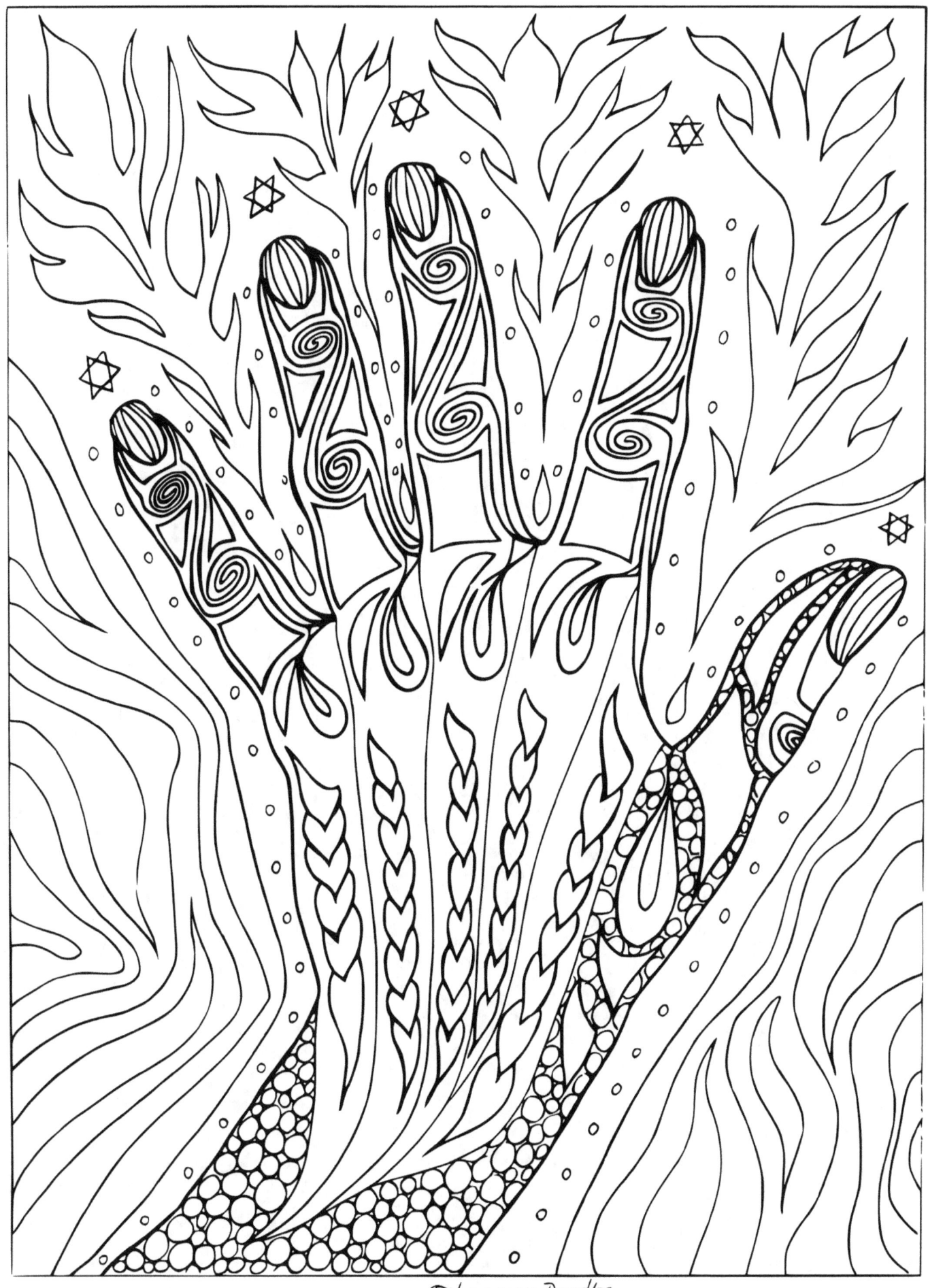

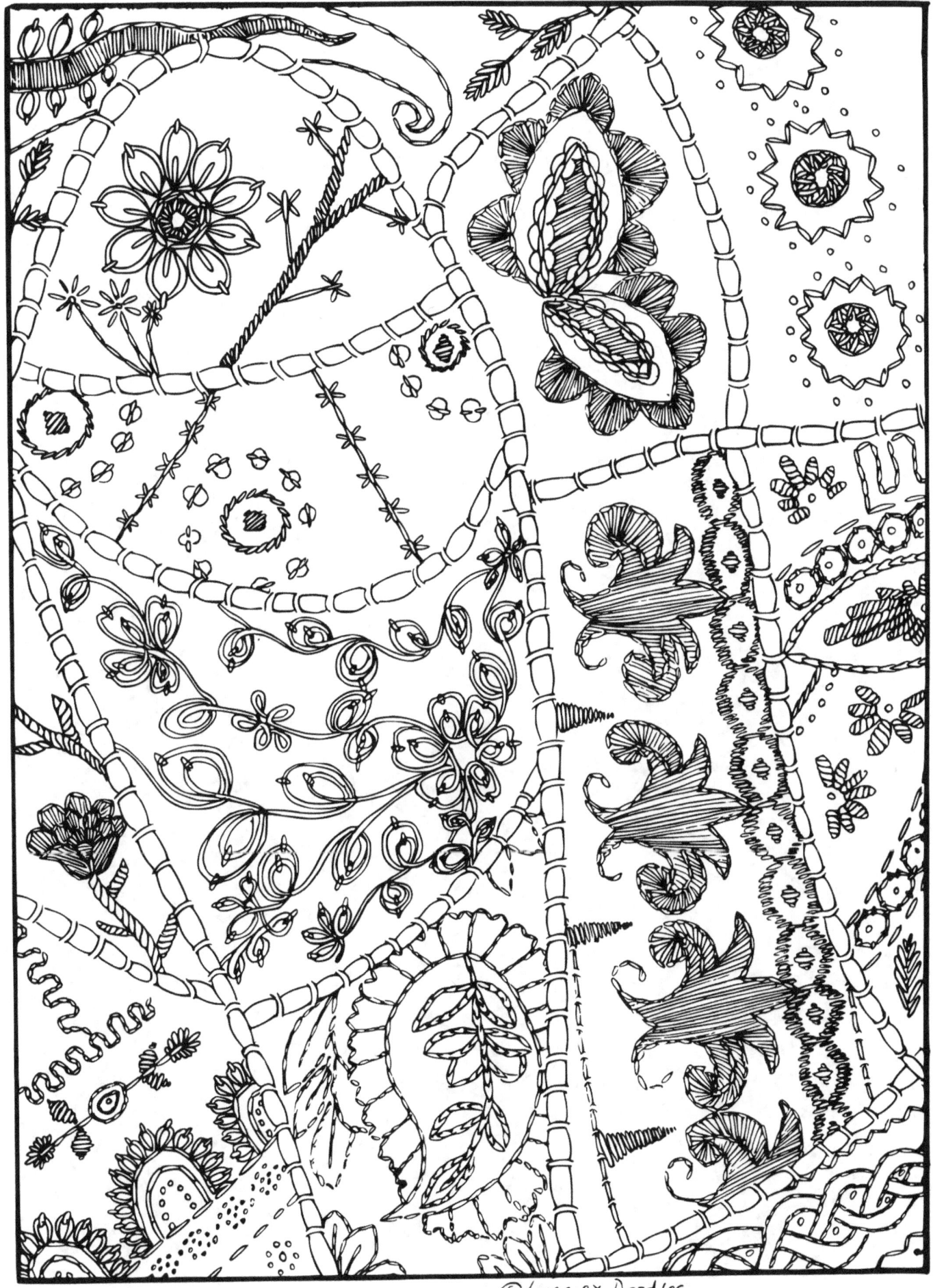

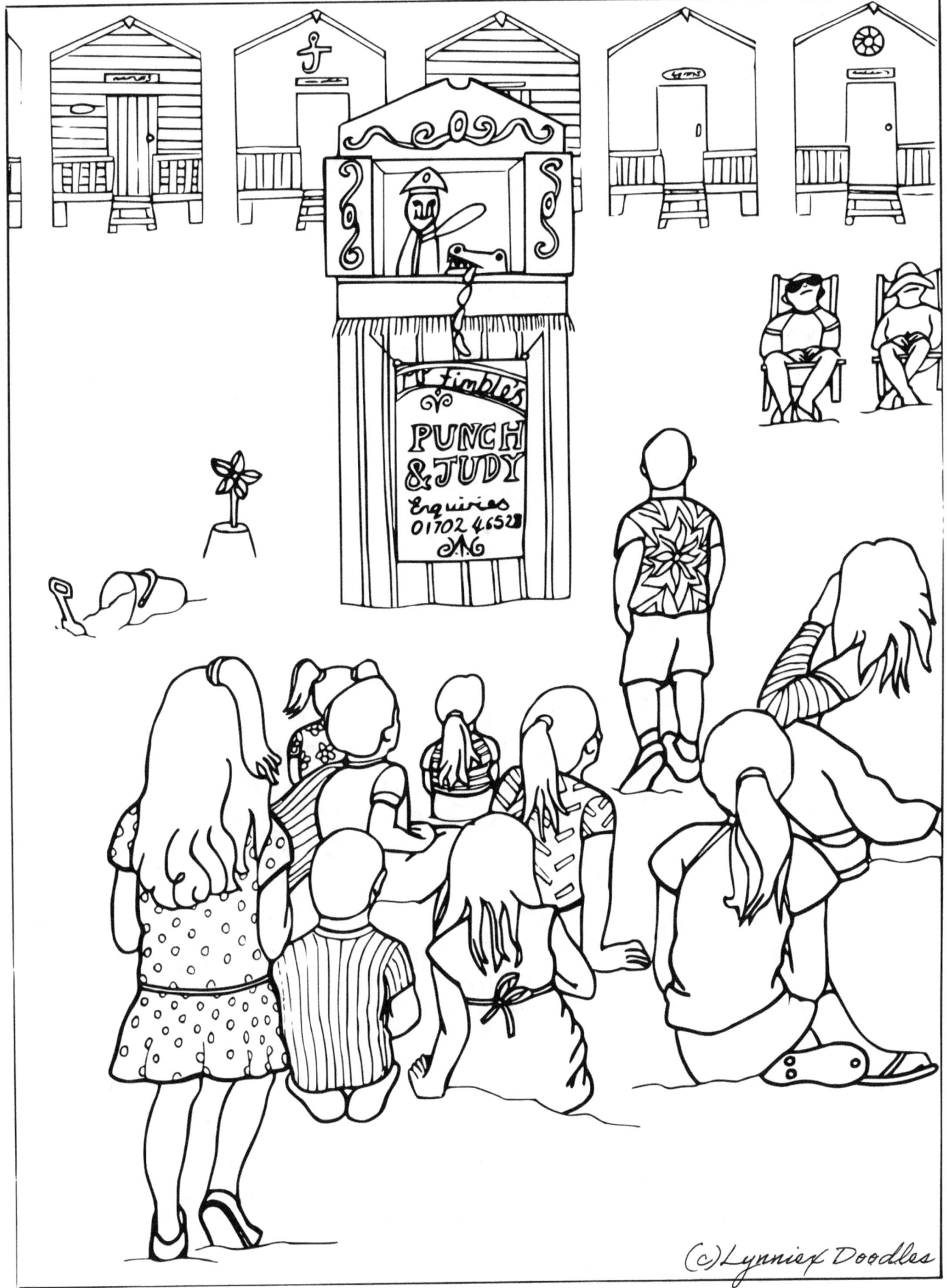

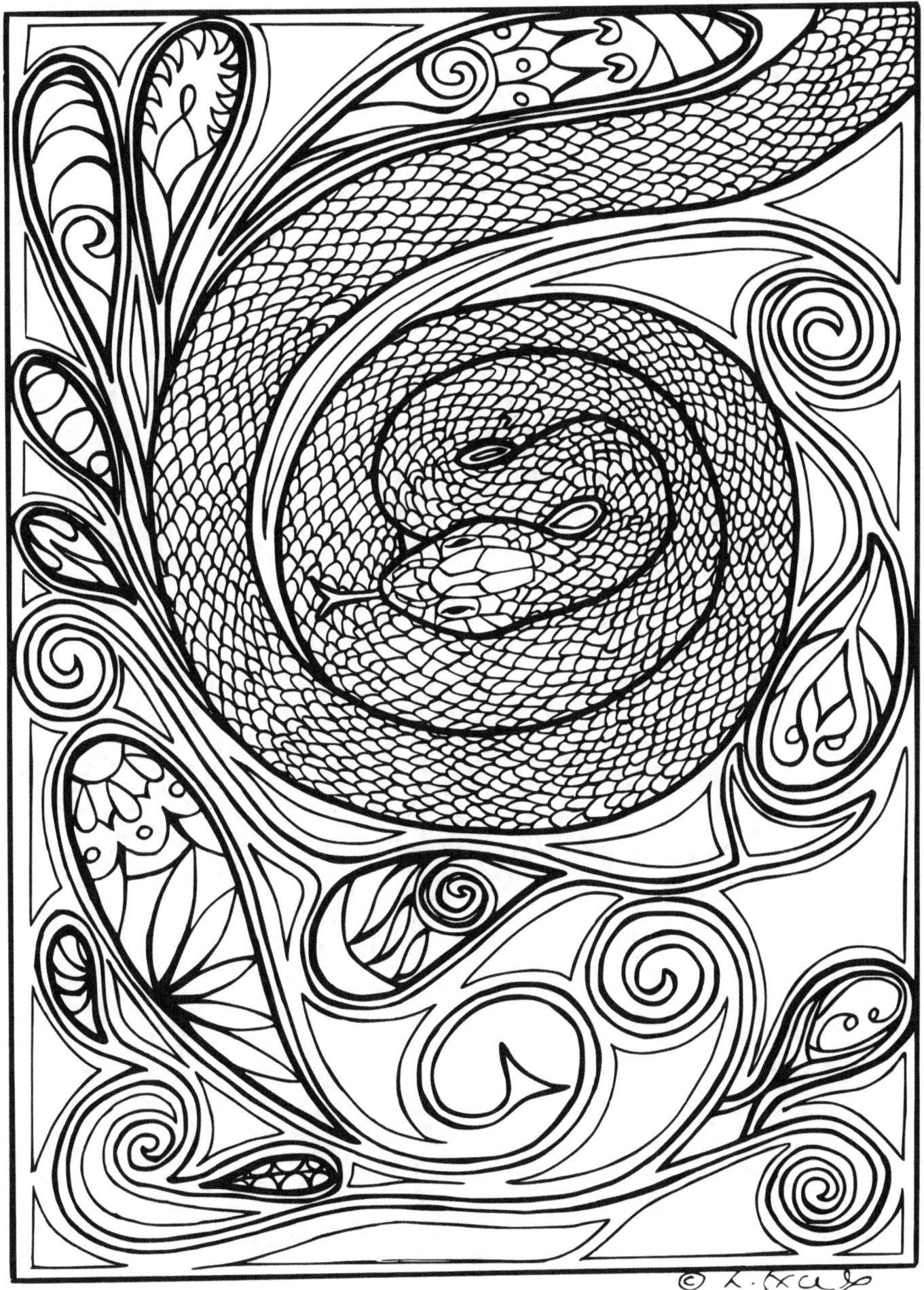

Chapter 2
Laurie Beauchamp
USA

Facebook : Lauries-Art

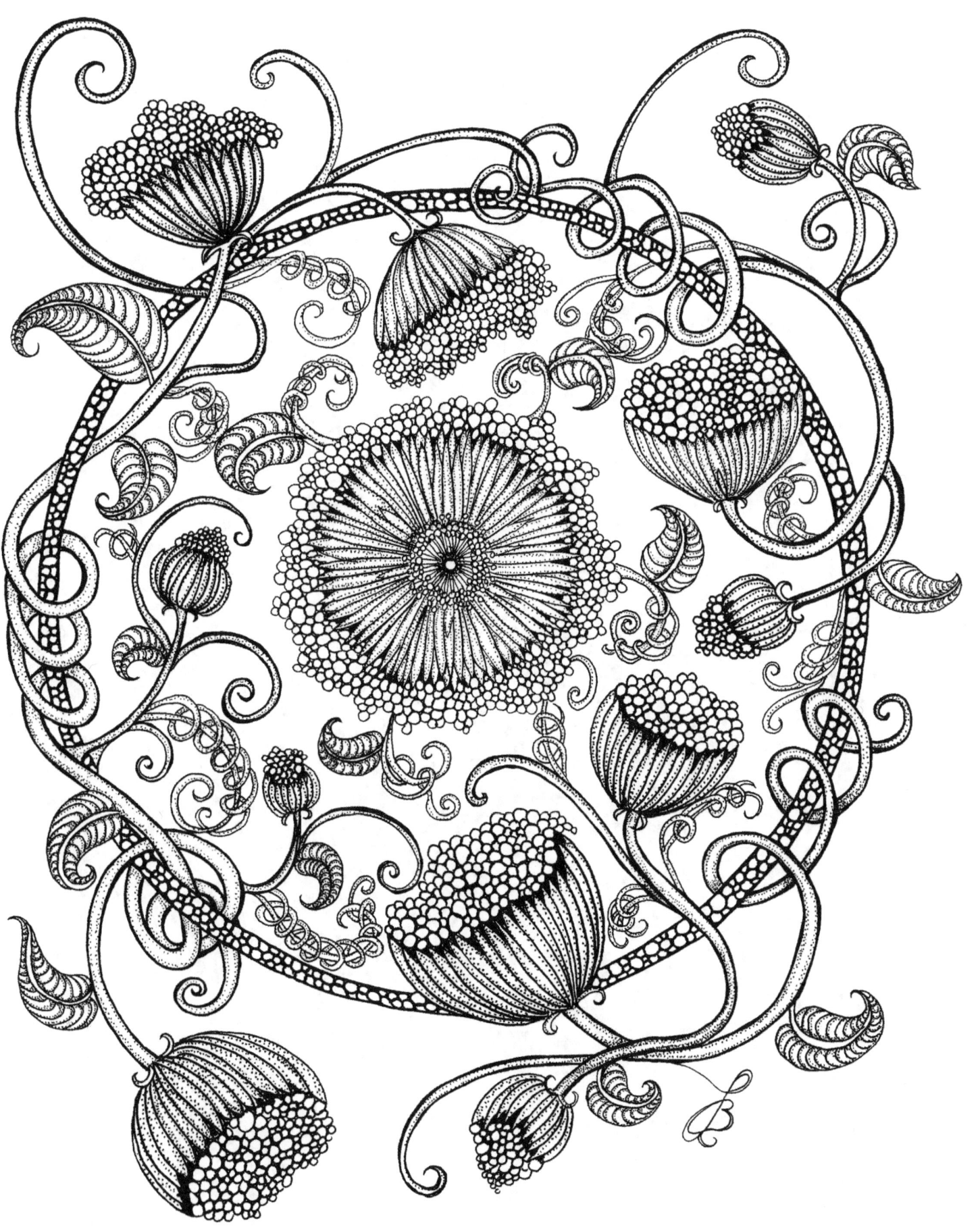

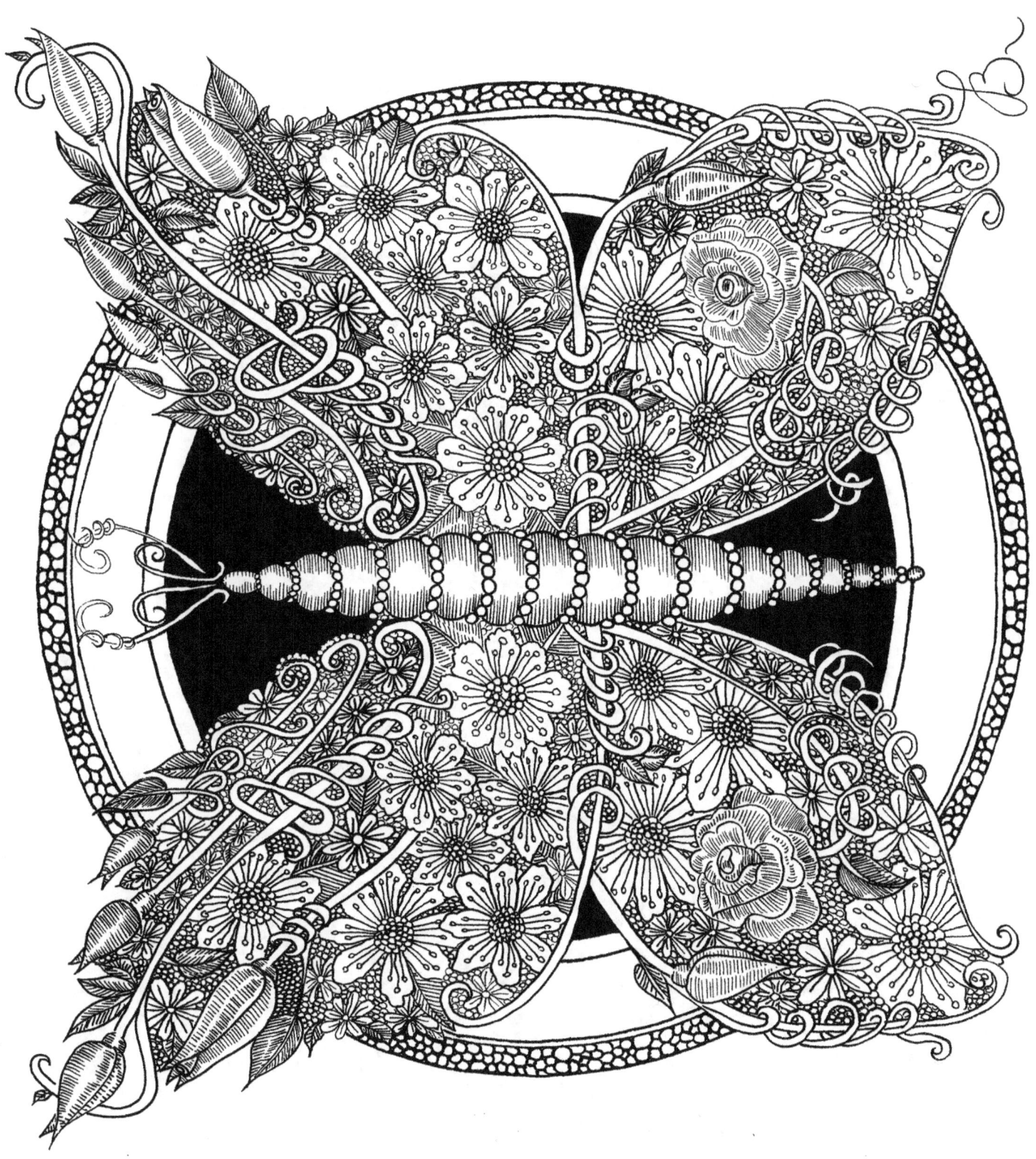

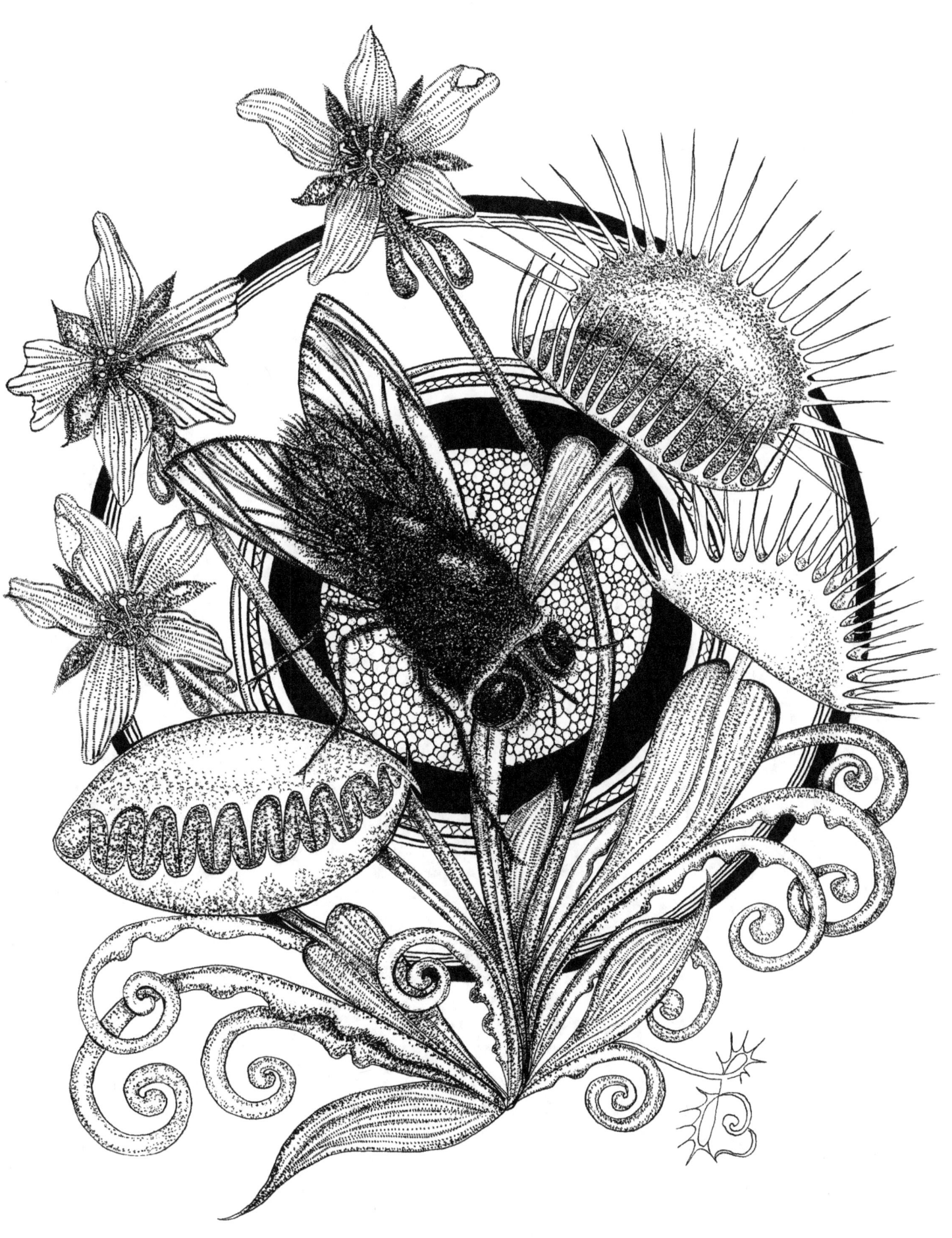

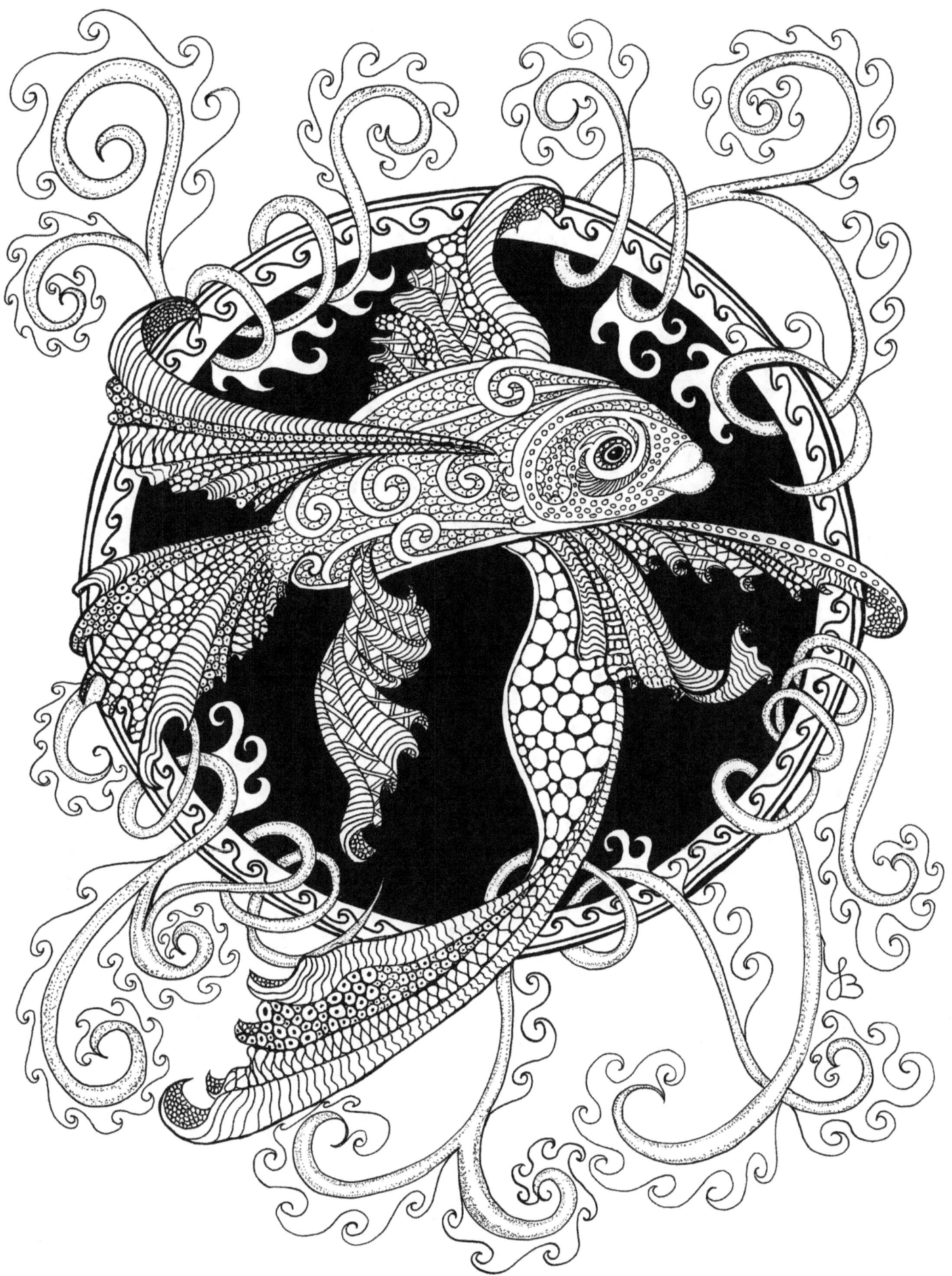

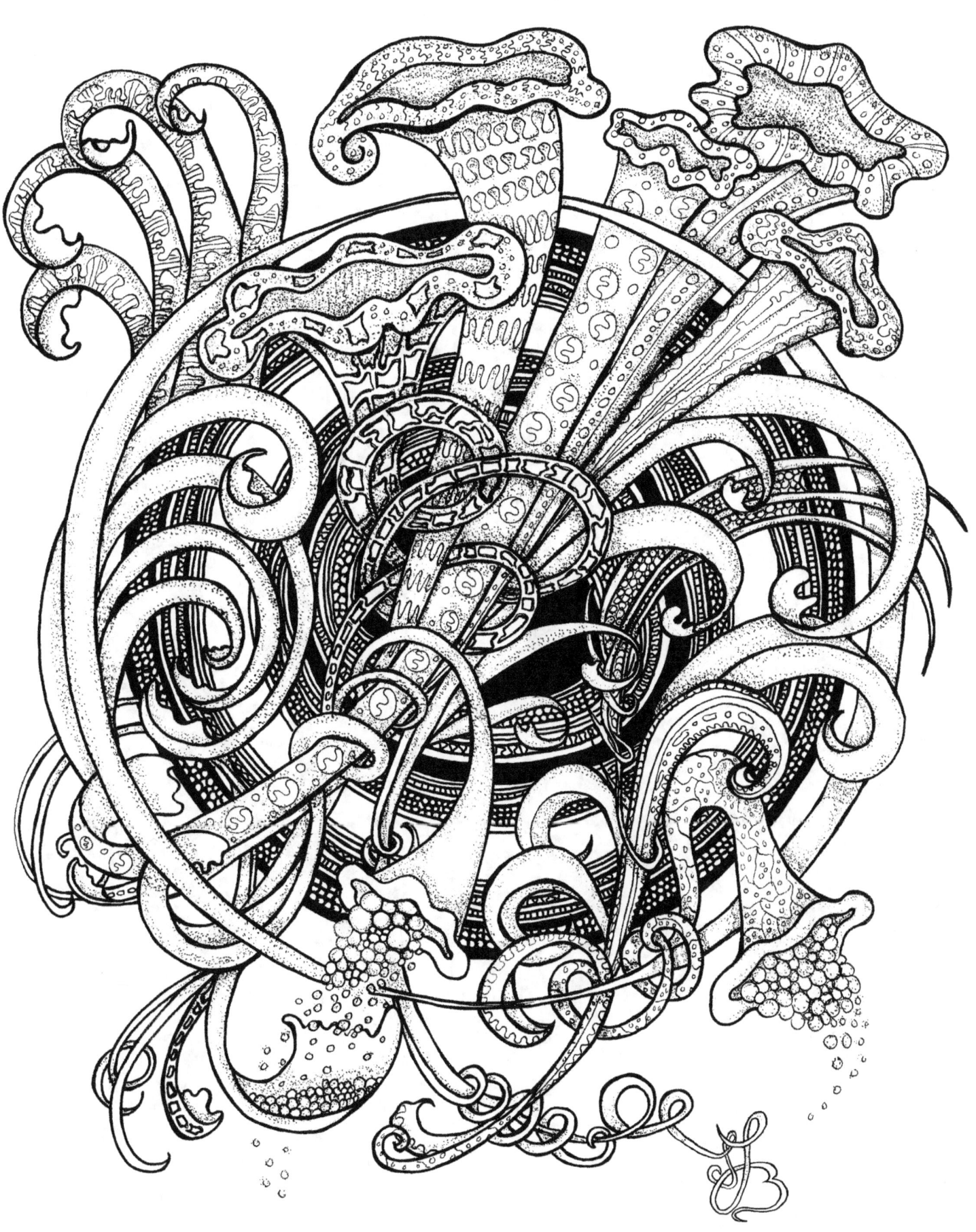

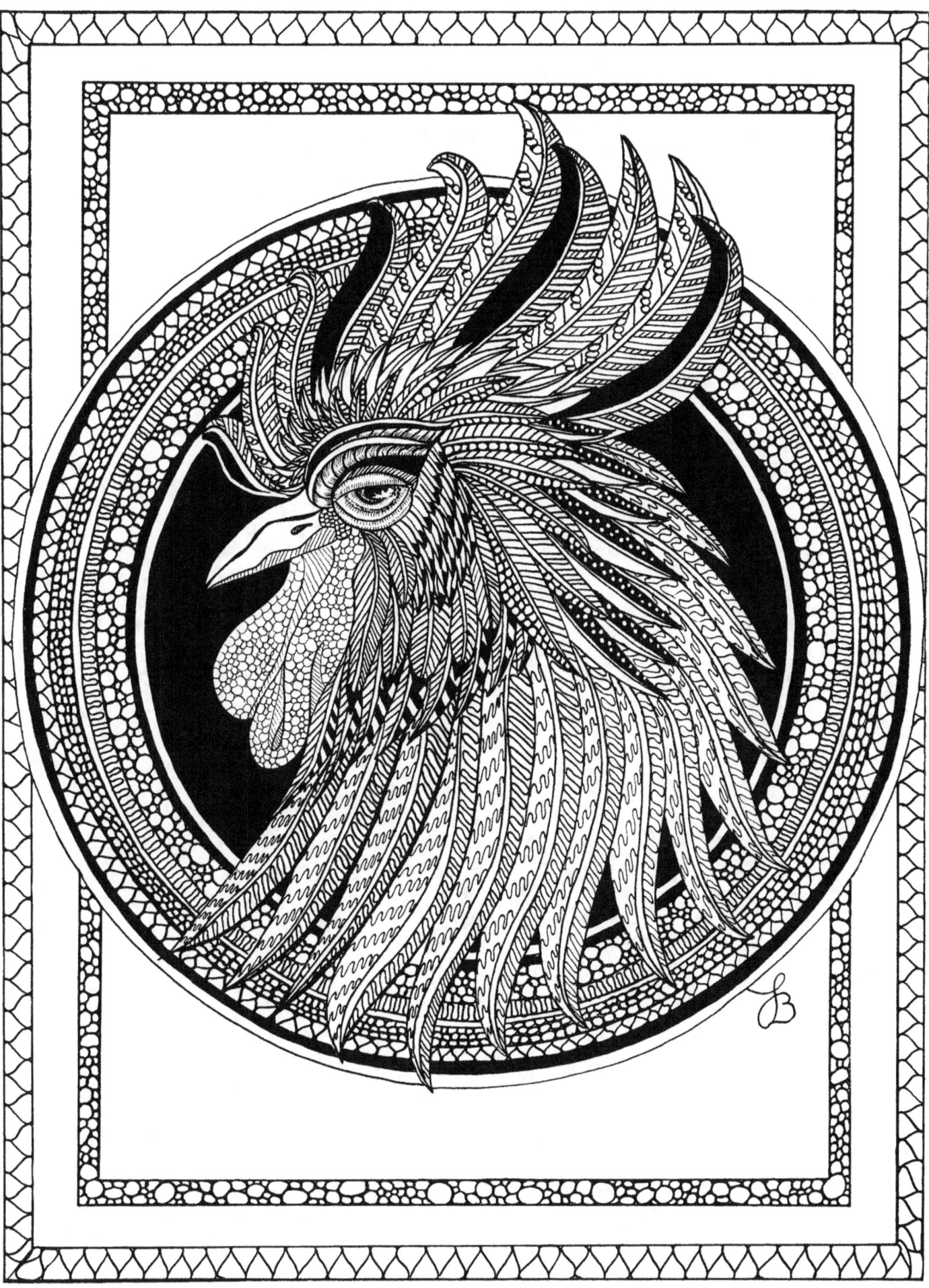

Chapter 3
Heather Richards
USA

Facebook : TangledTidbits

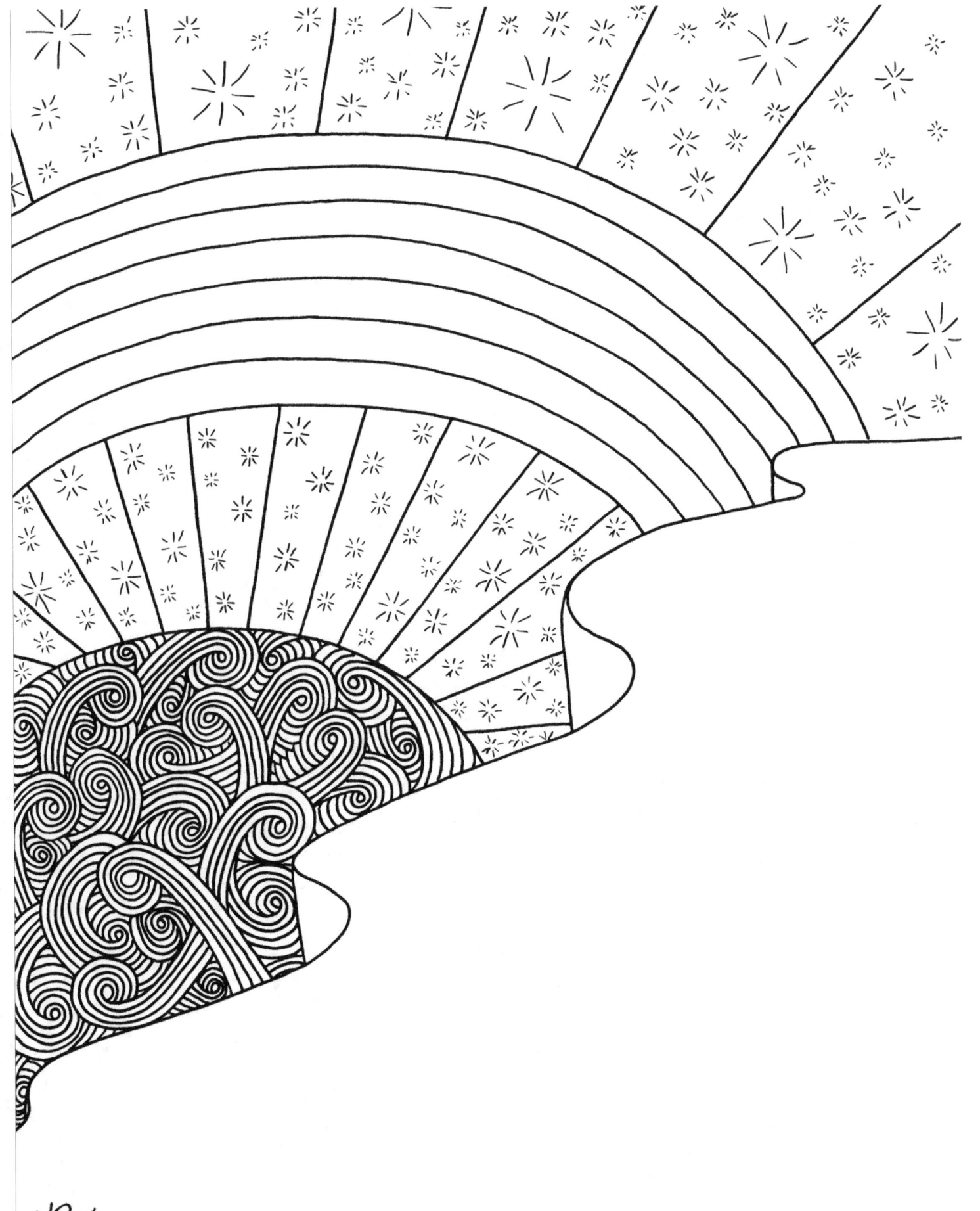

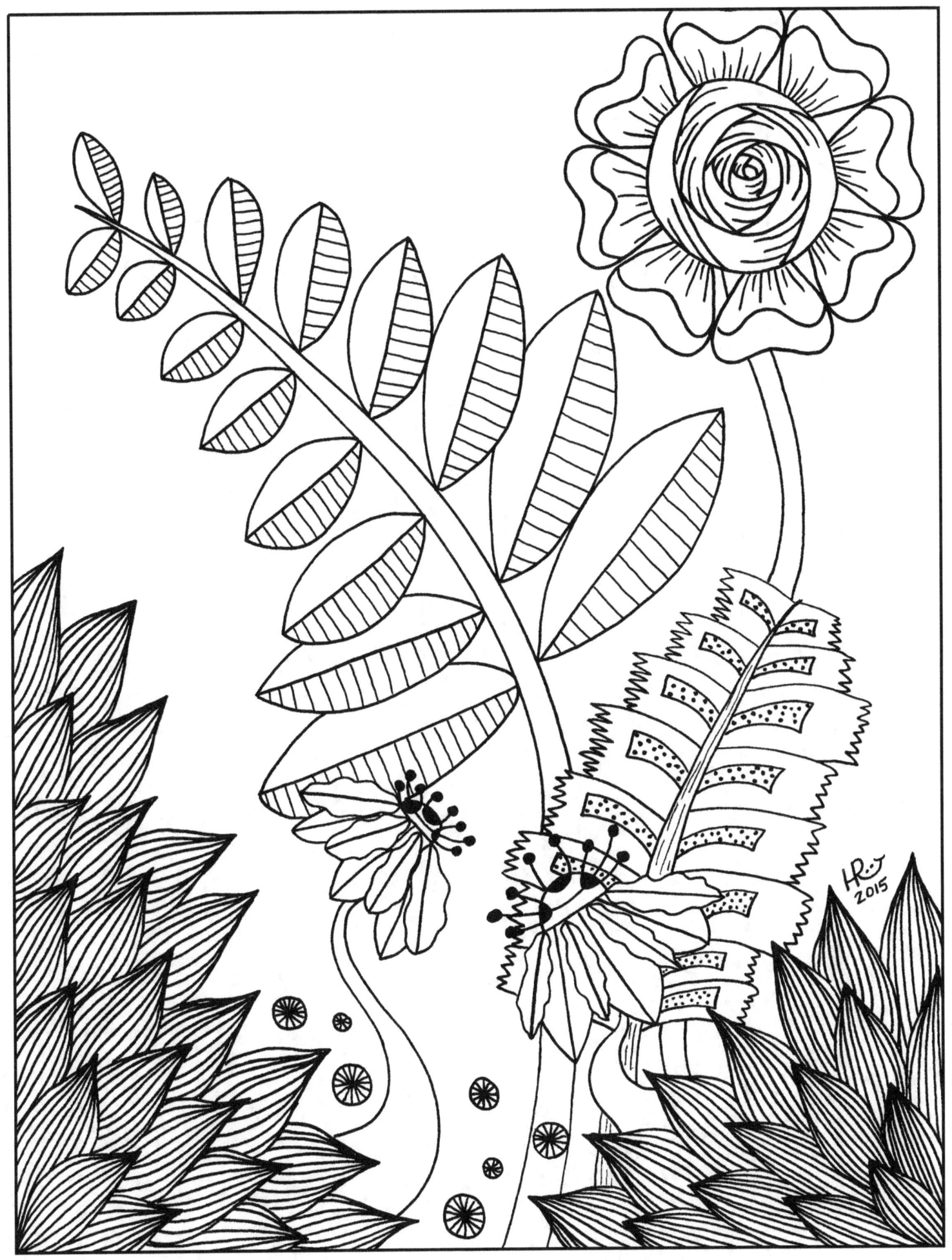

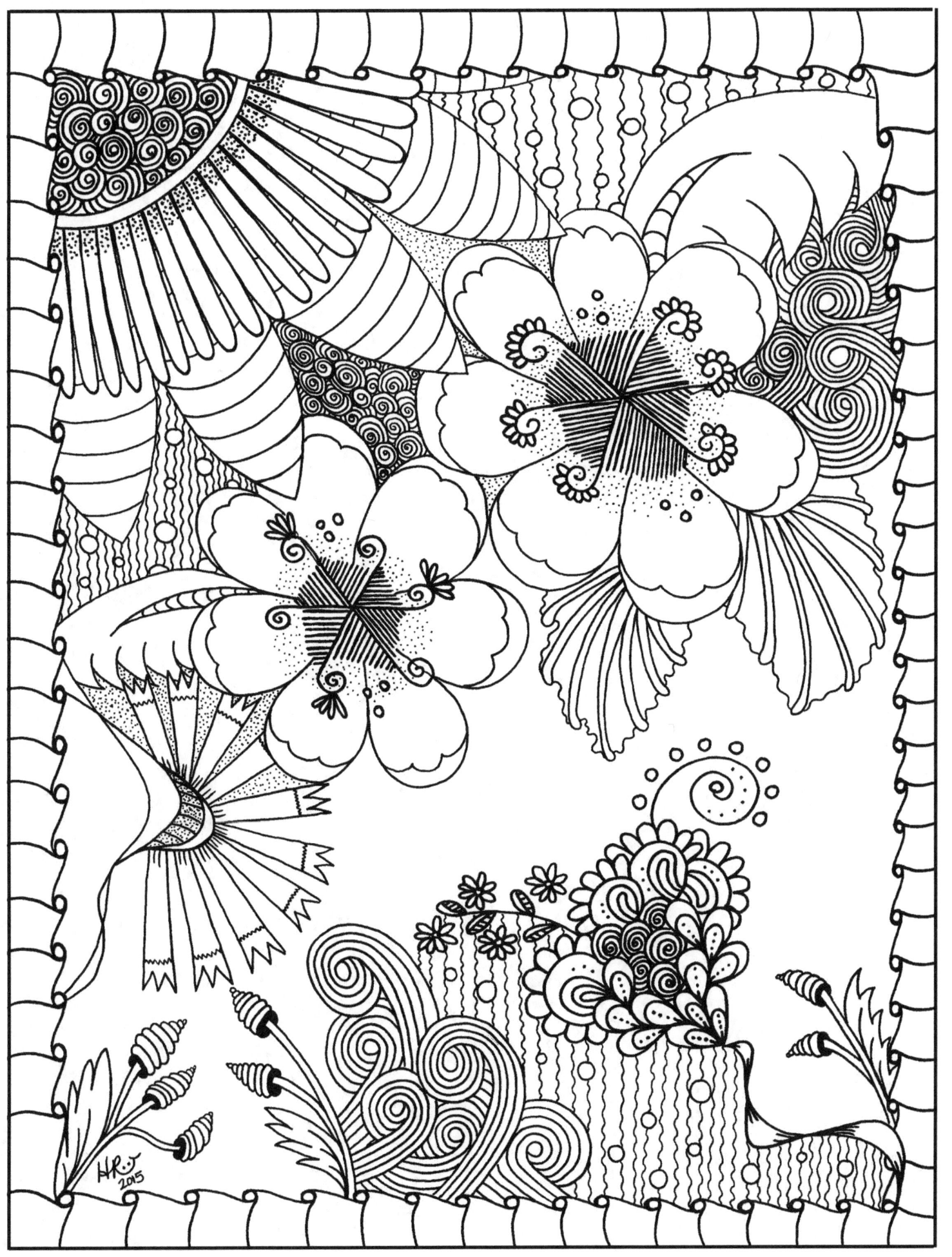

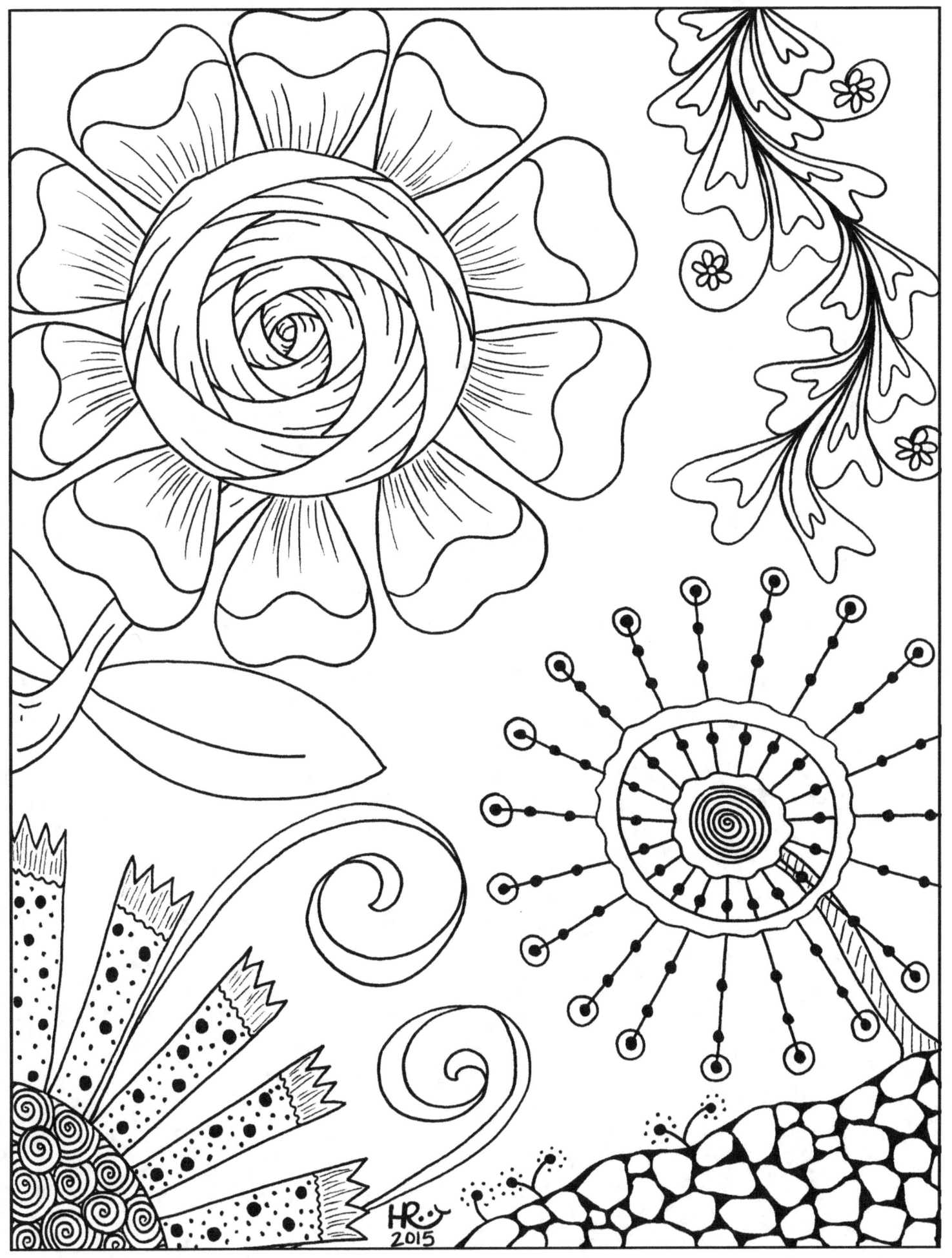

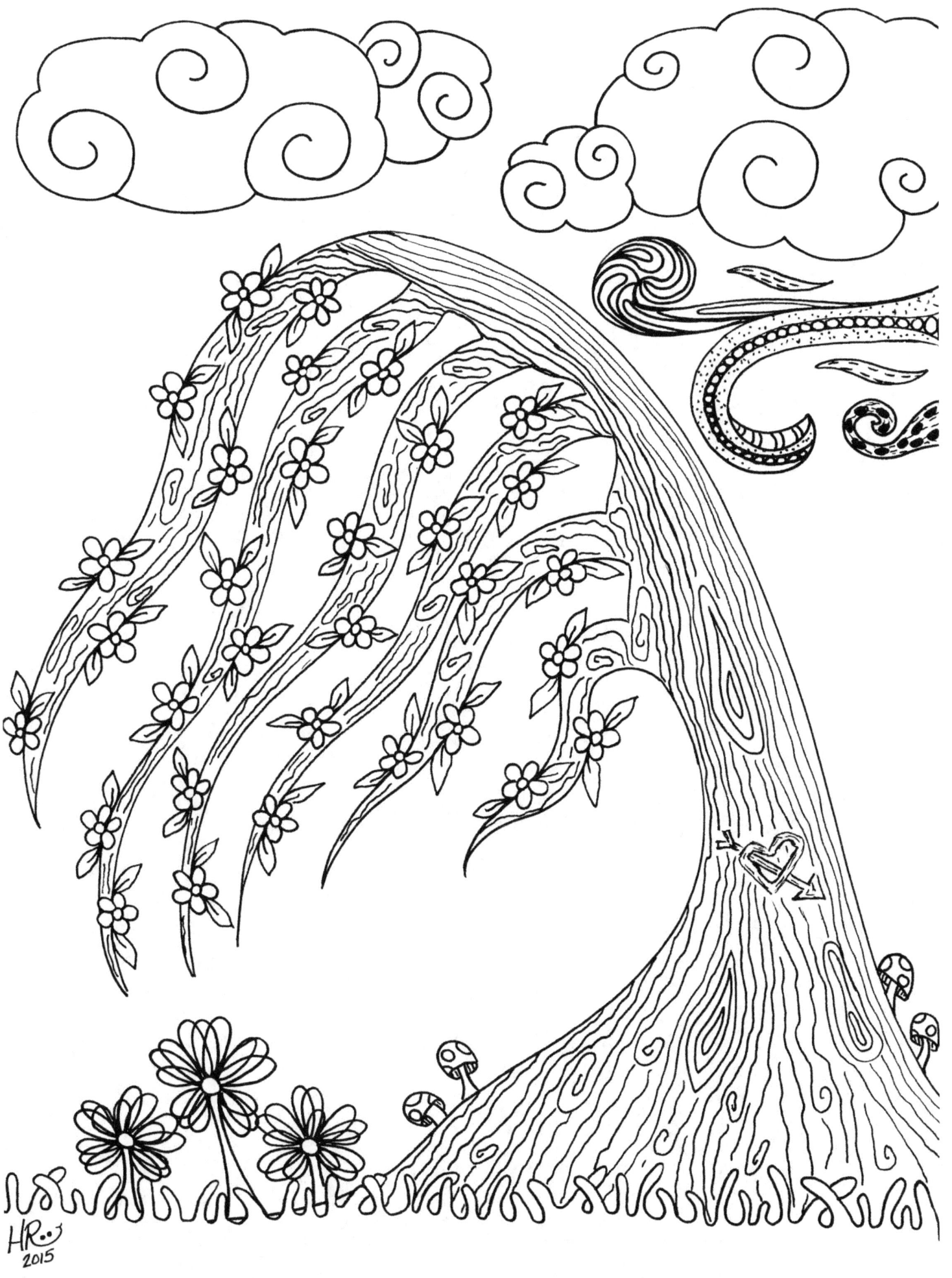

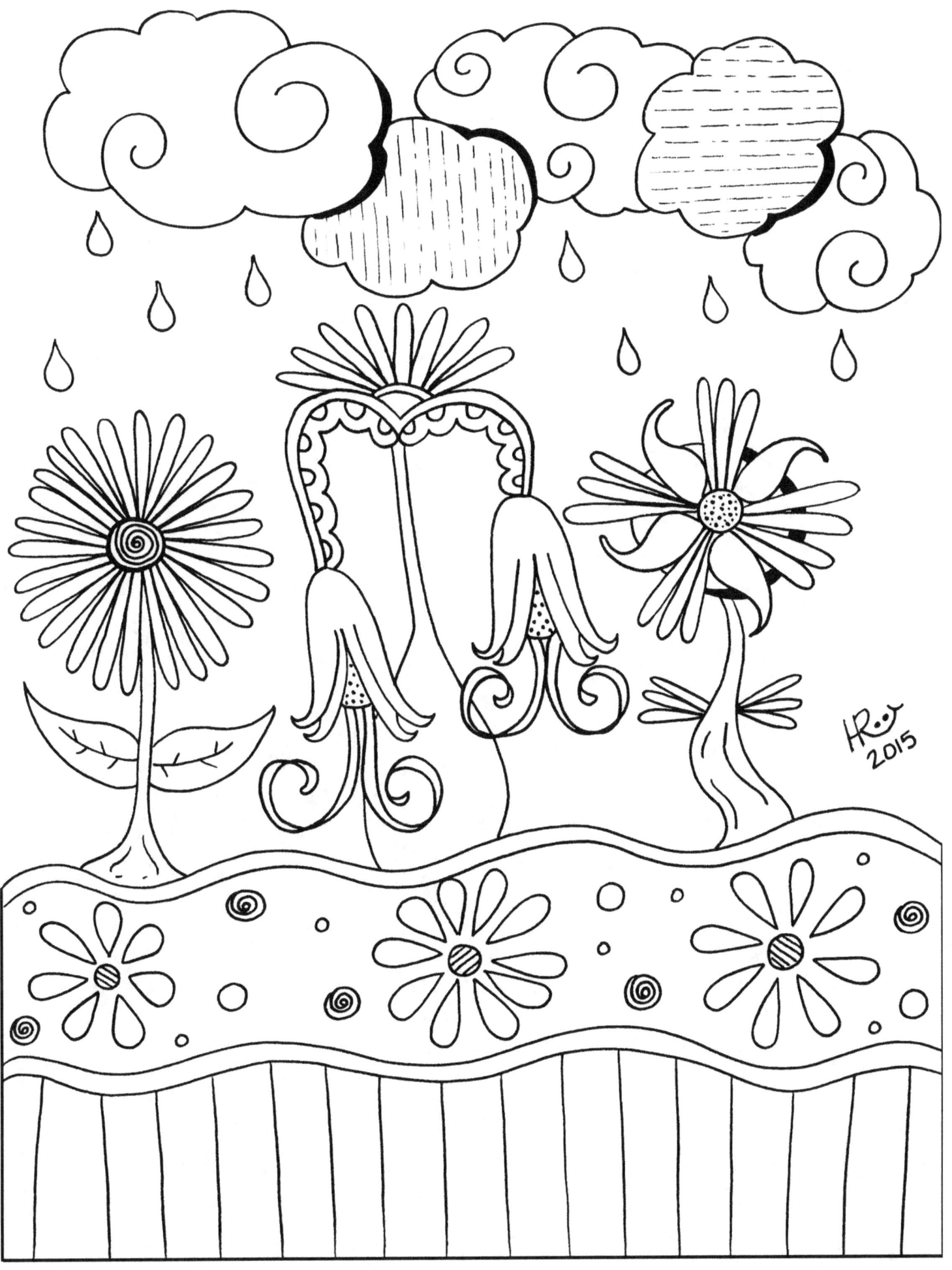

Chapter 4
Nicole Whelan
USA

Facebook : NicoleWhelanArt

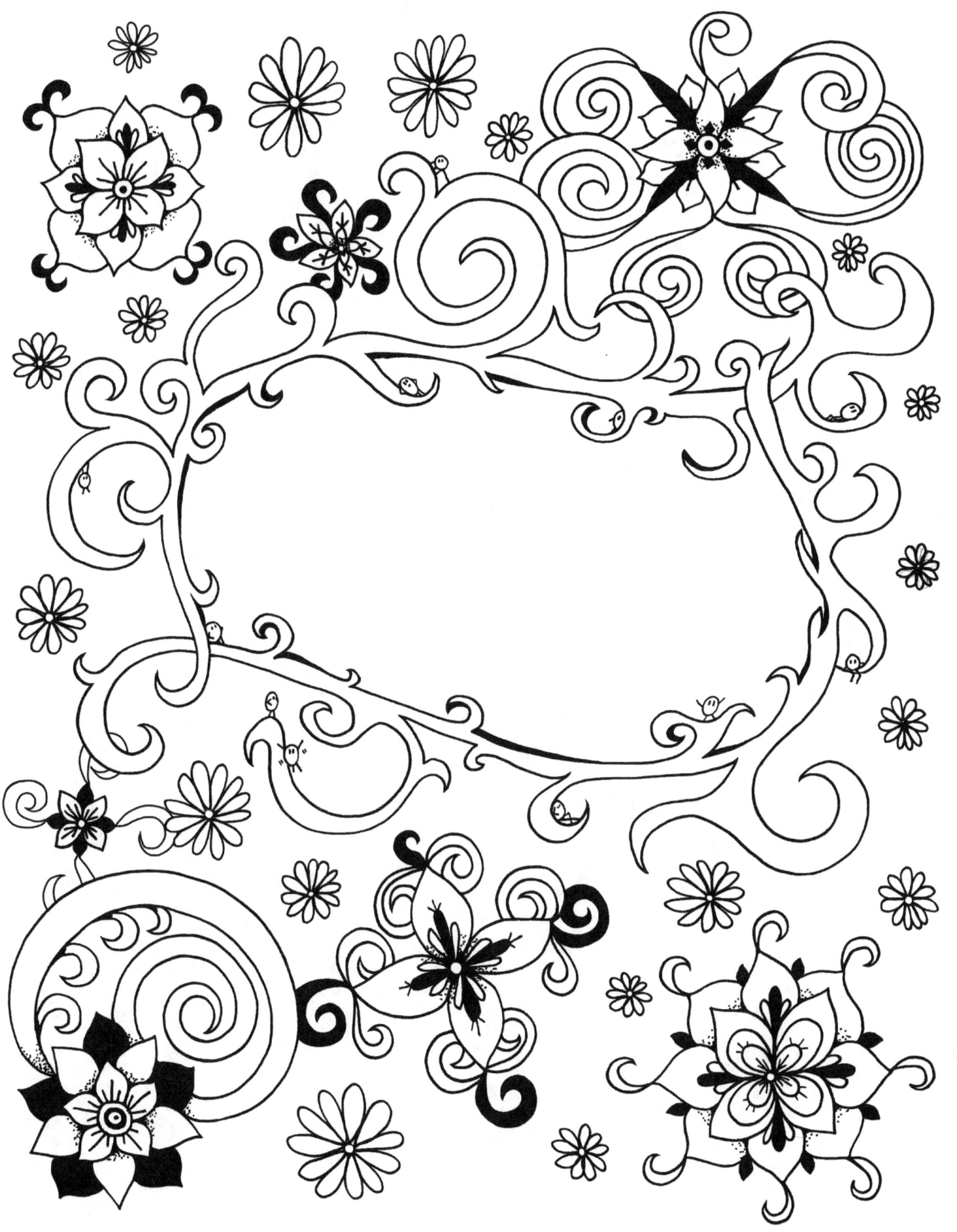

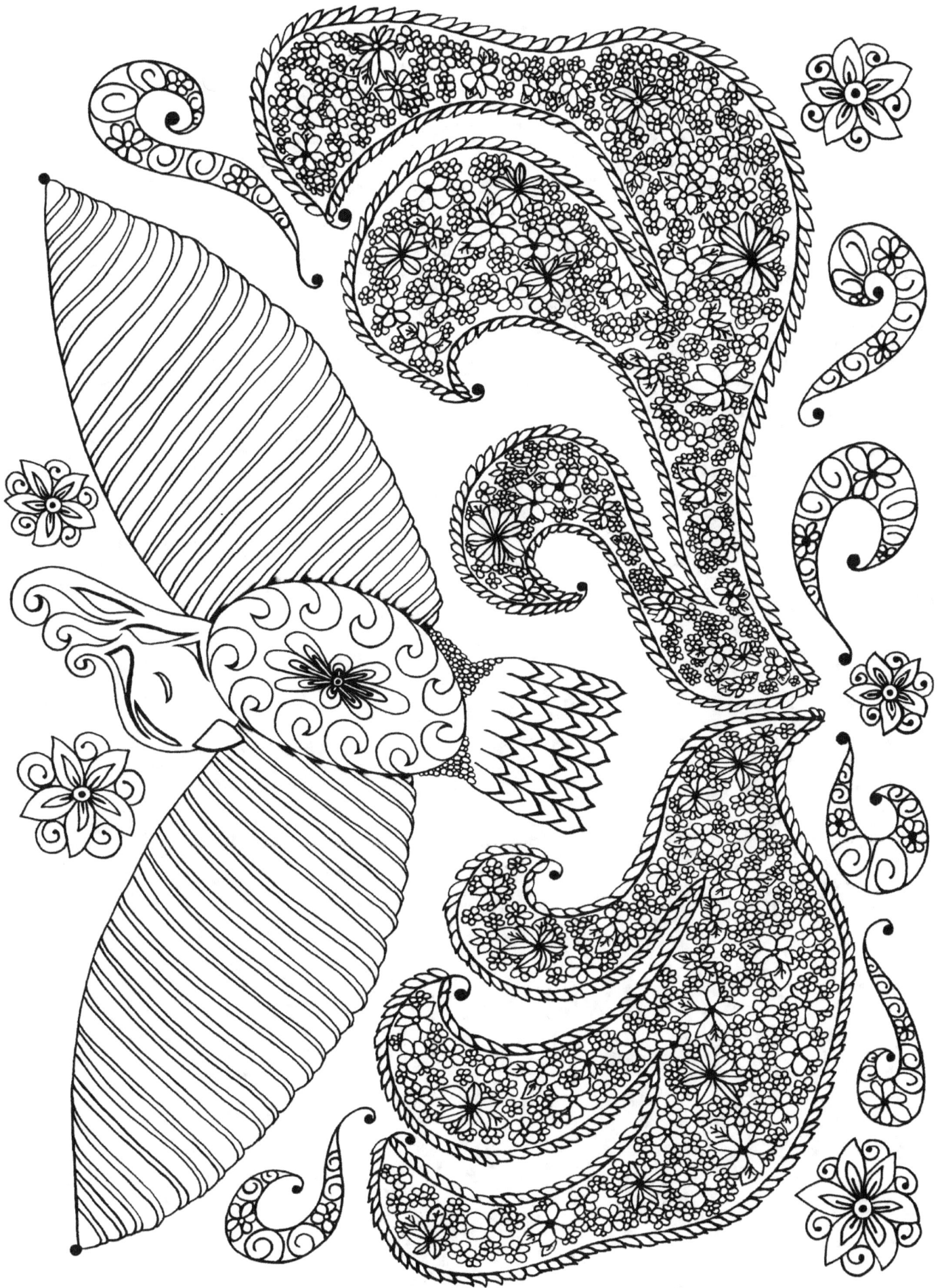

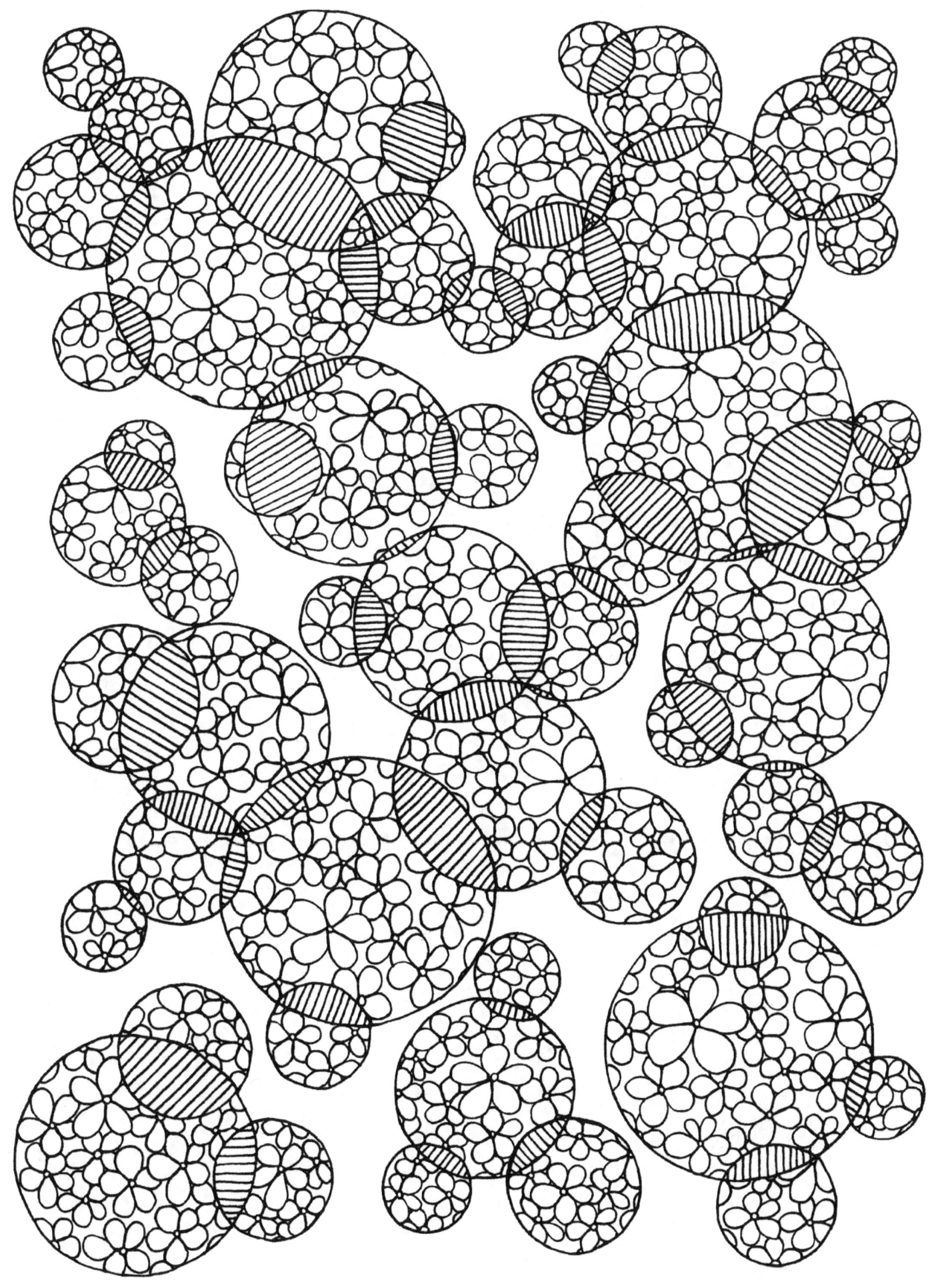

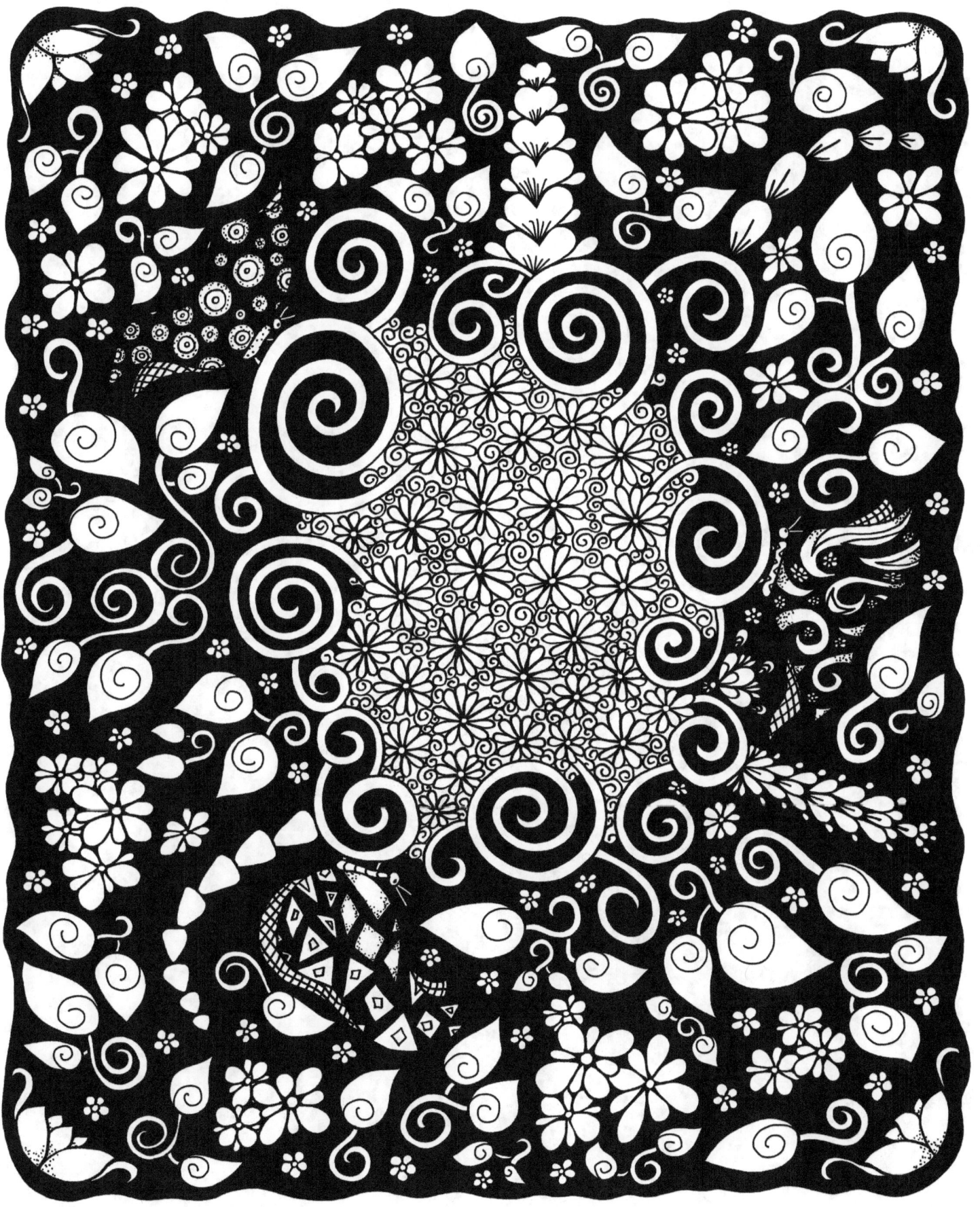

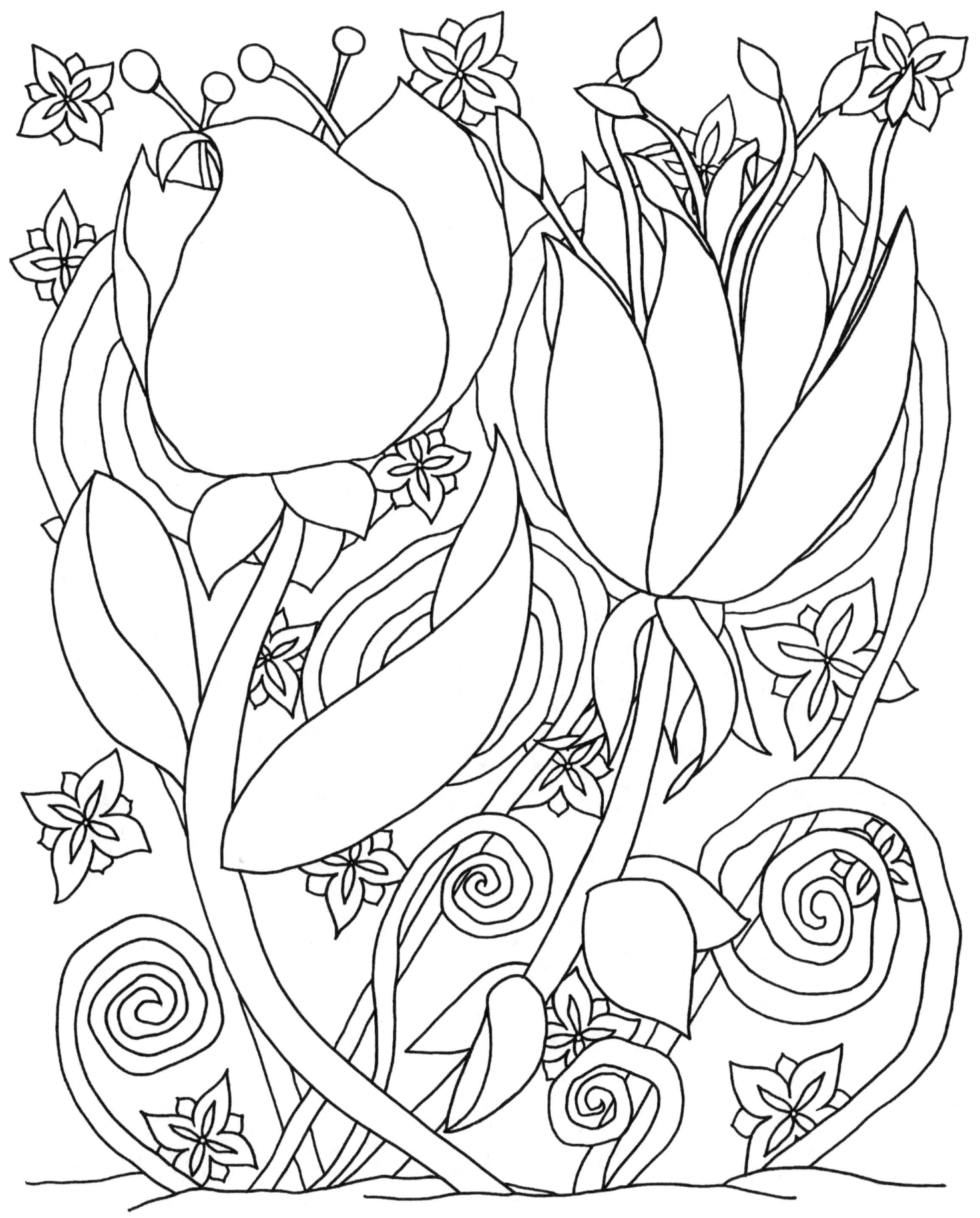

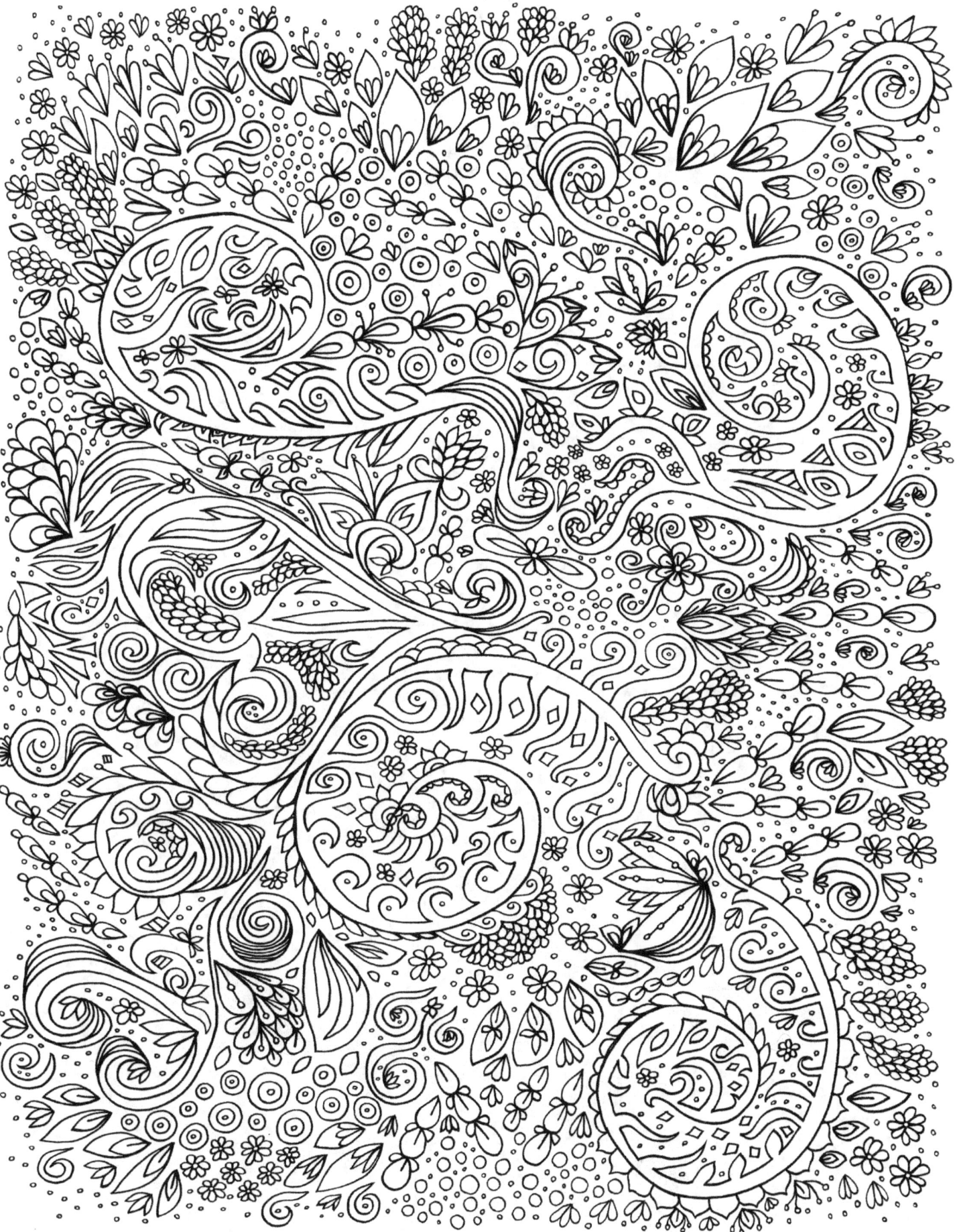

Chapter 5
Cathy M.
France

Facebook : EdgArtStudio
http://www.edg-studio.net

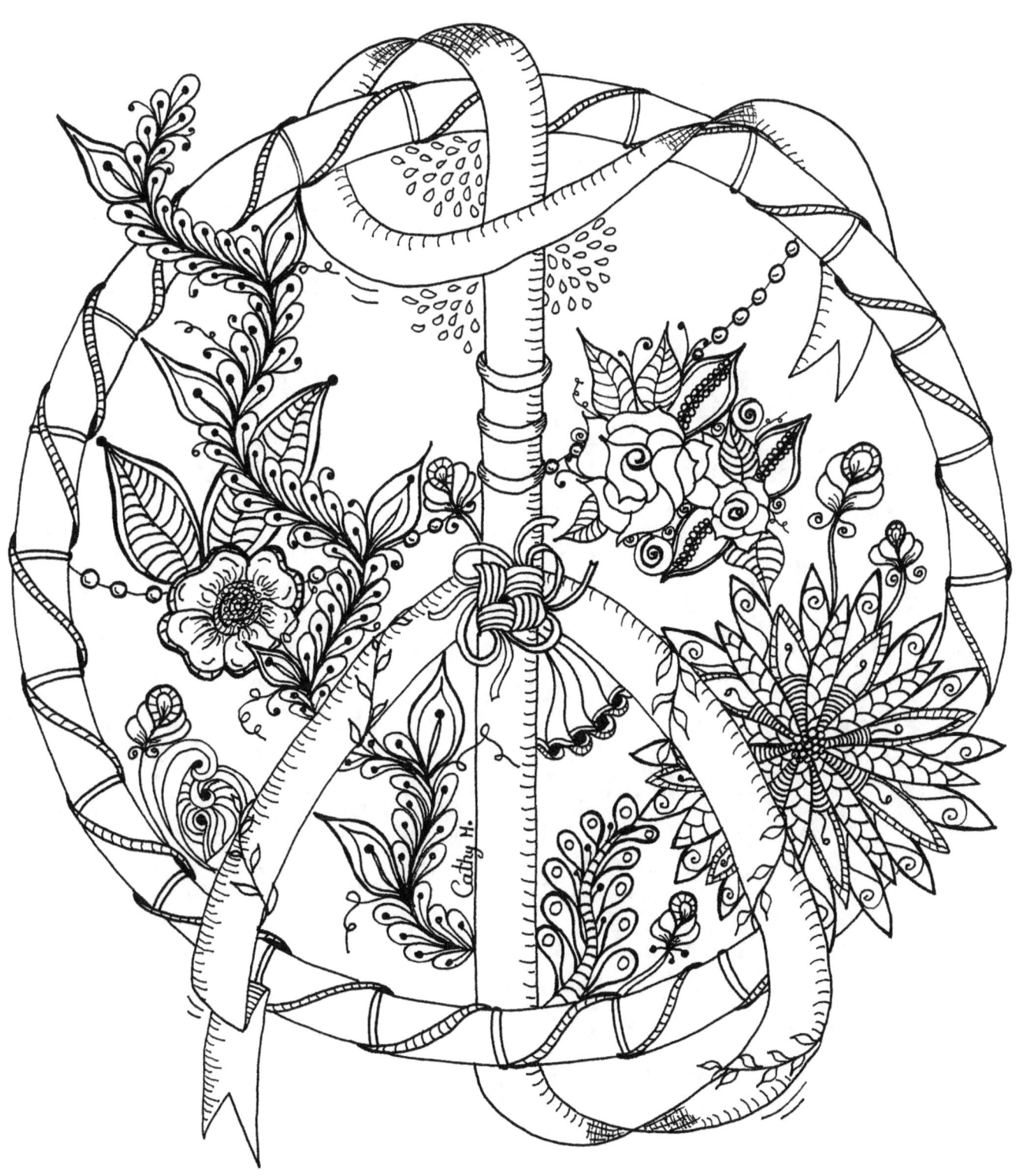

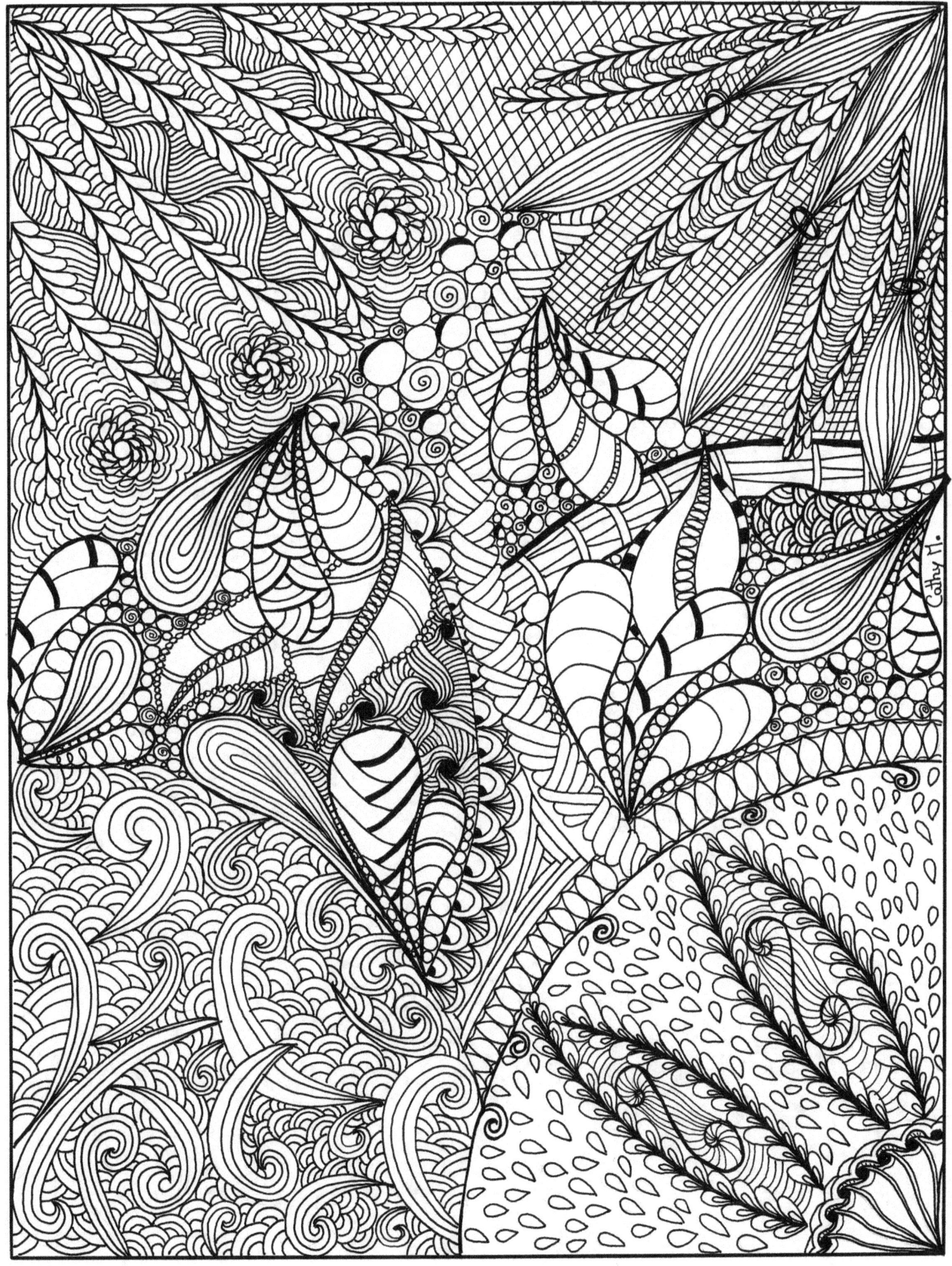

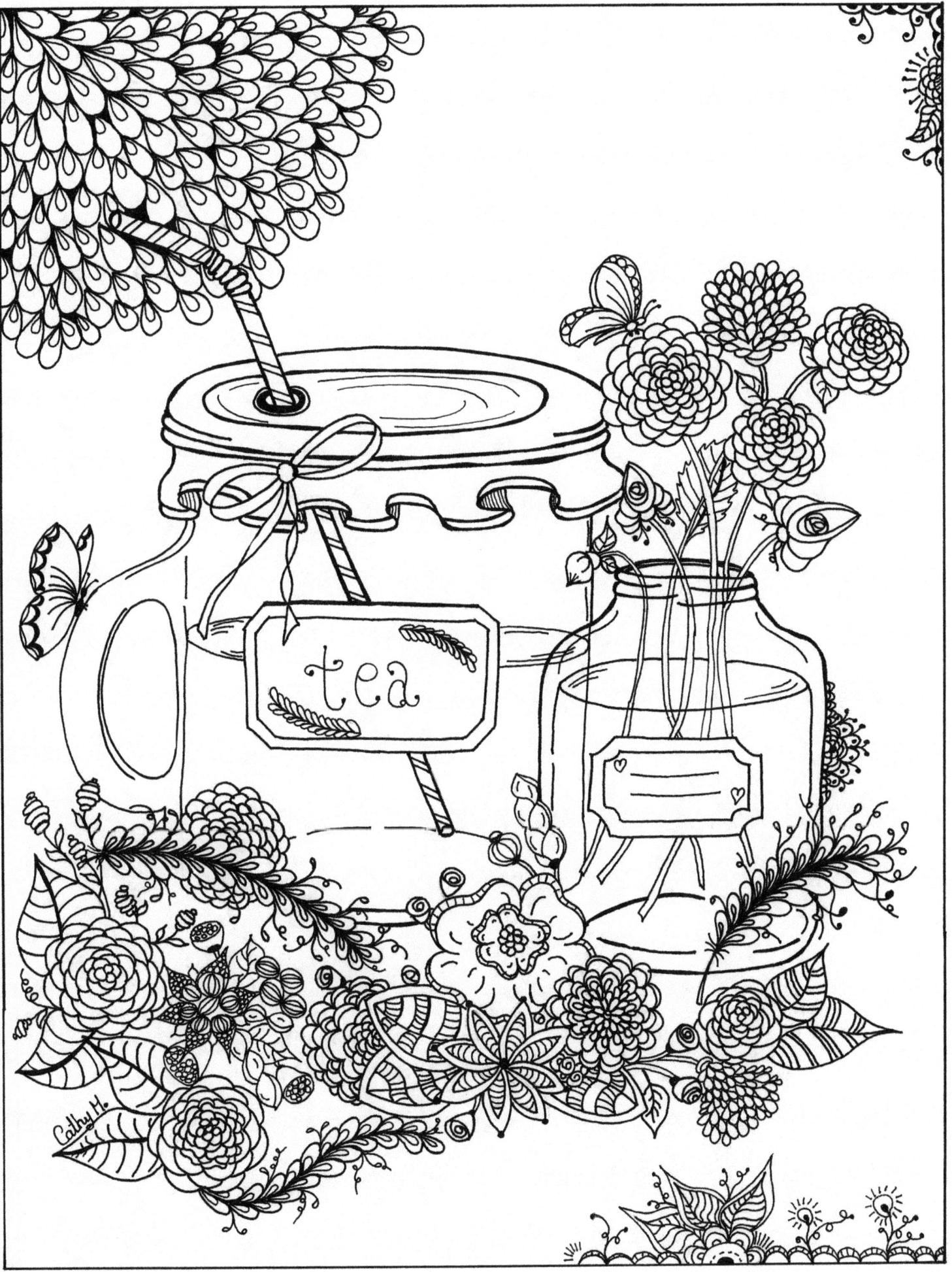

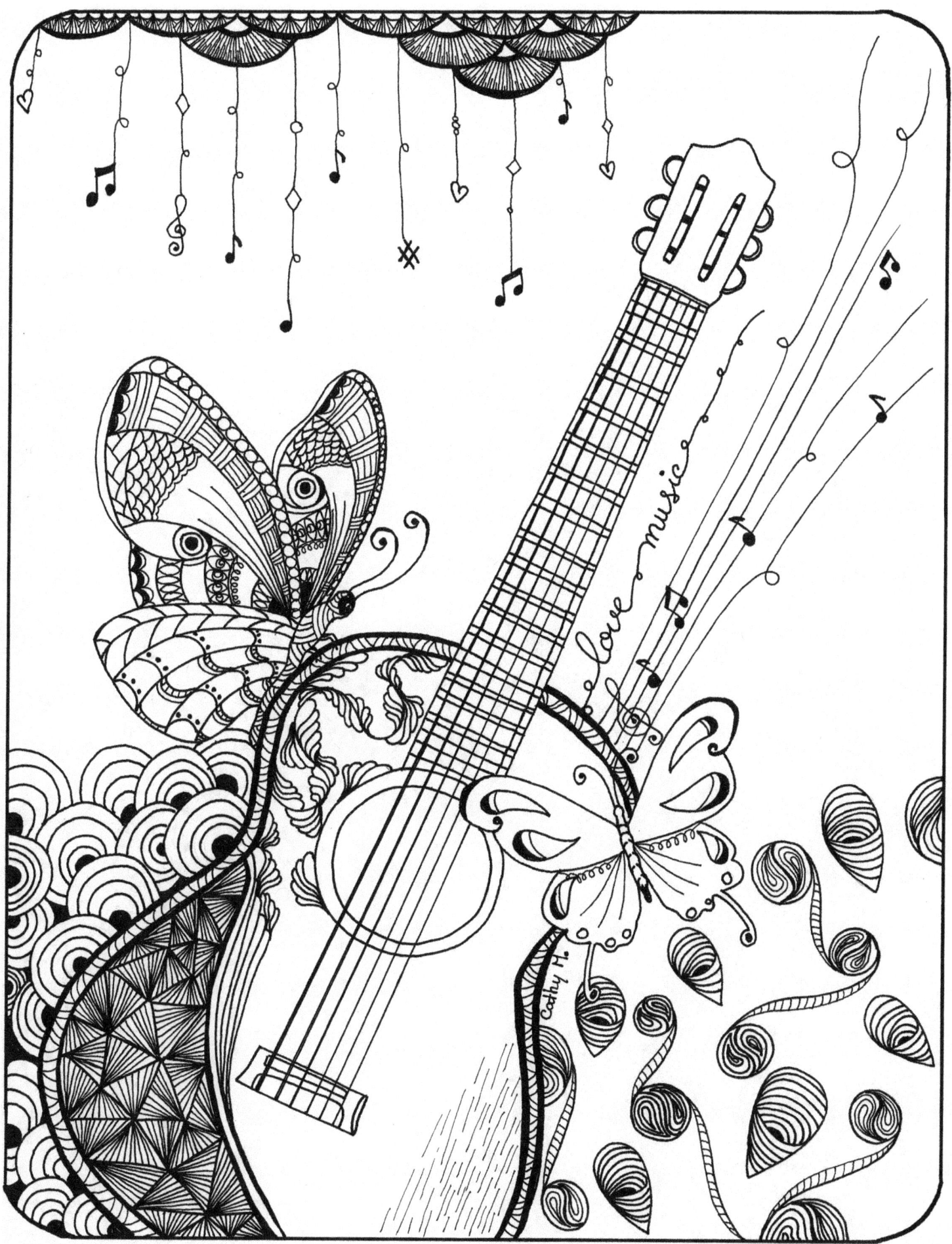

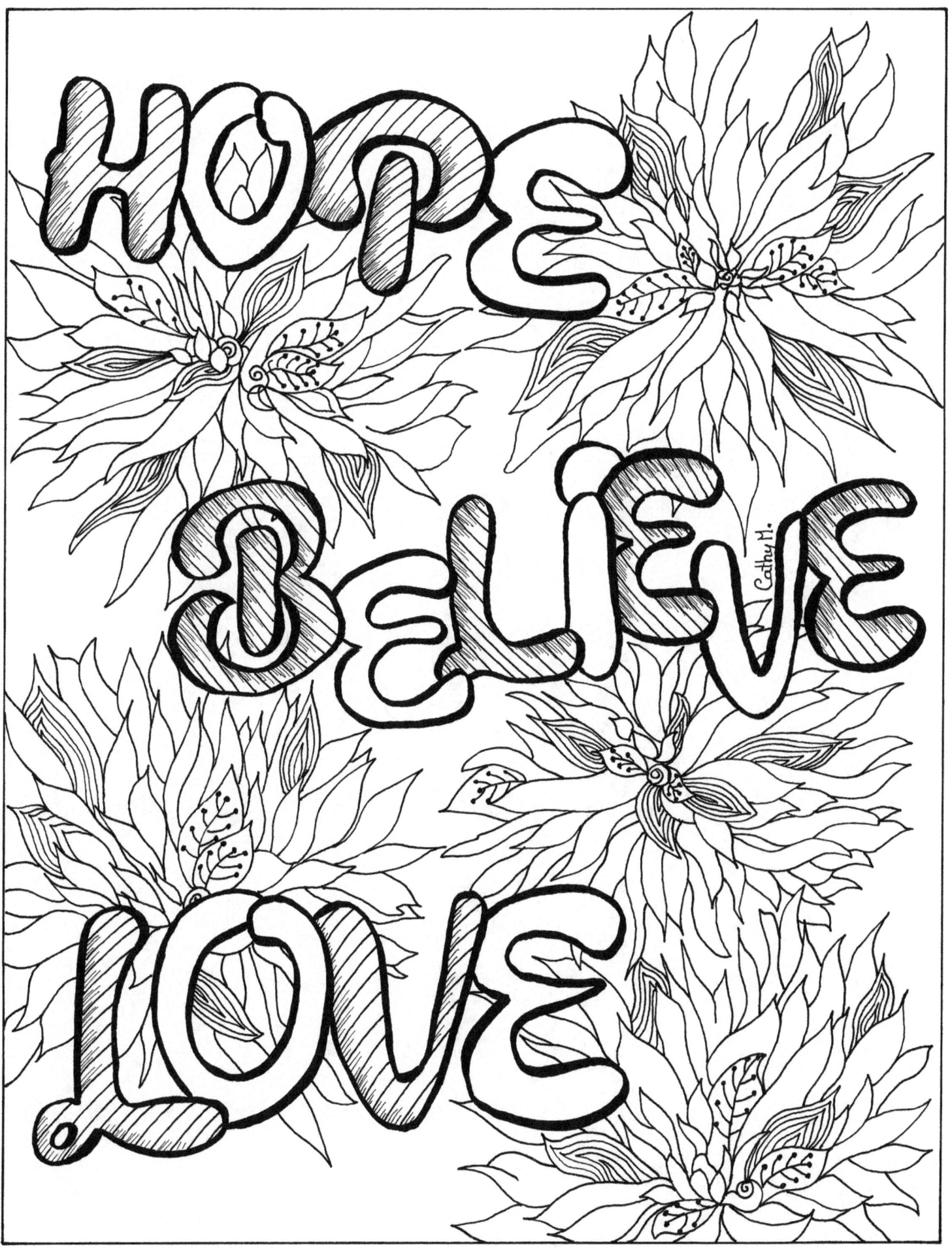

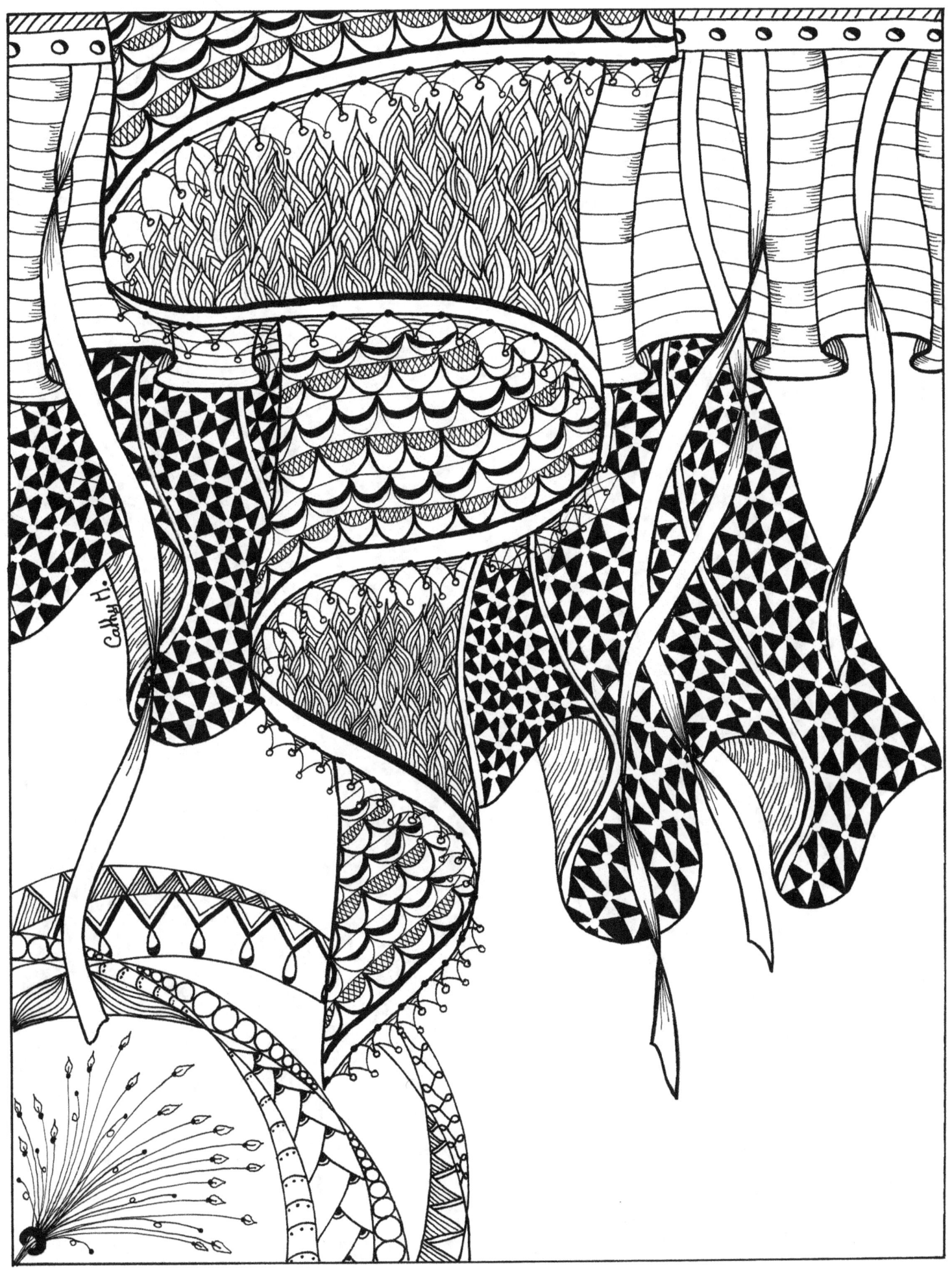

Chapter 6
Leen Margot
France

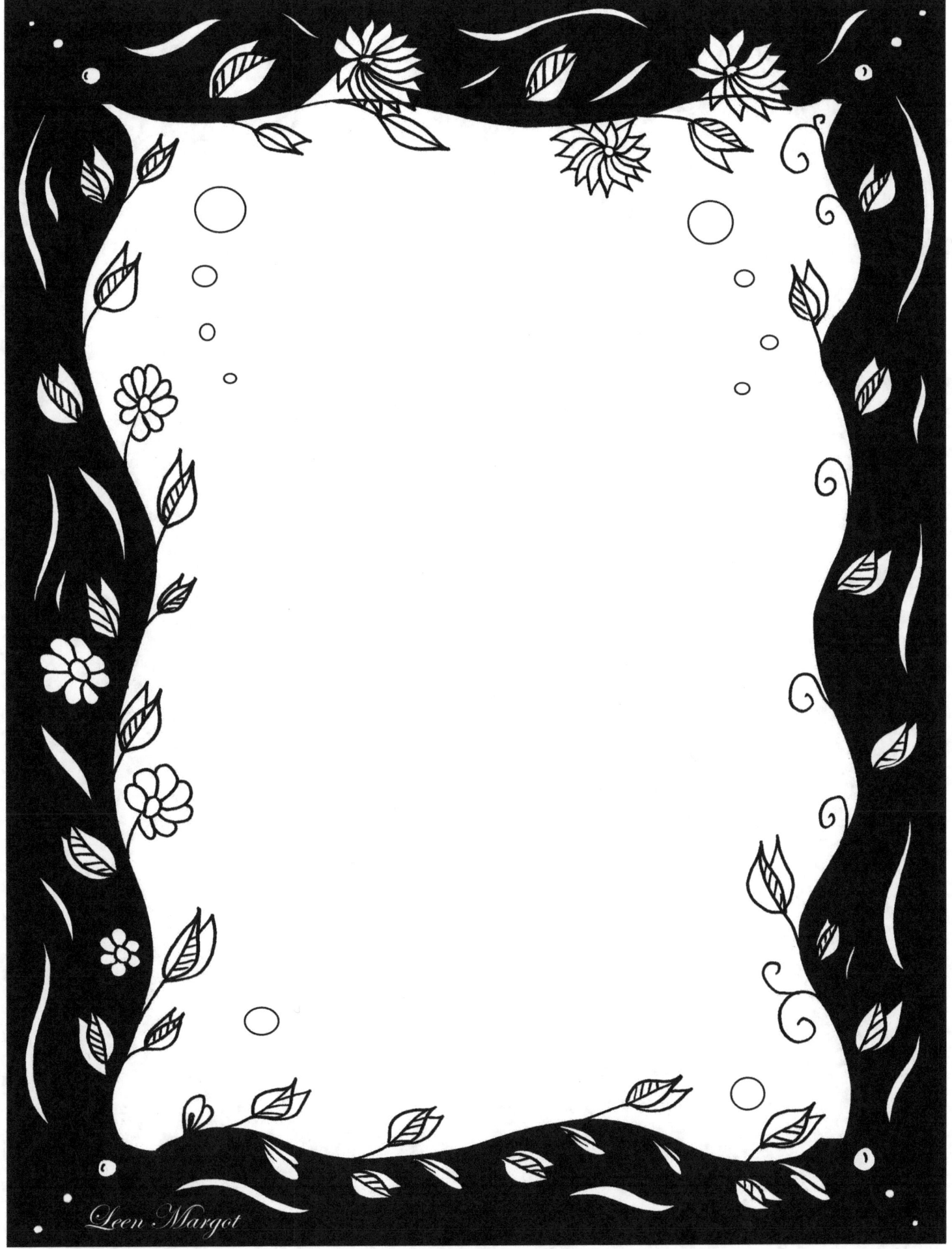

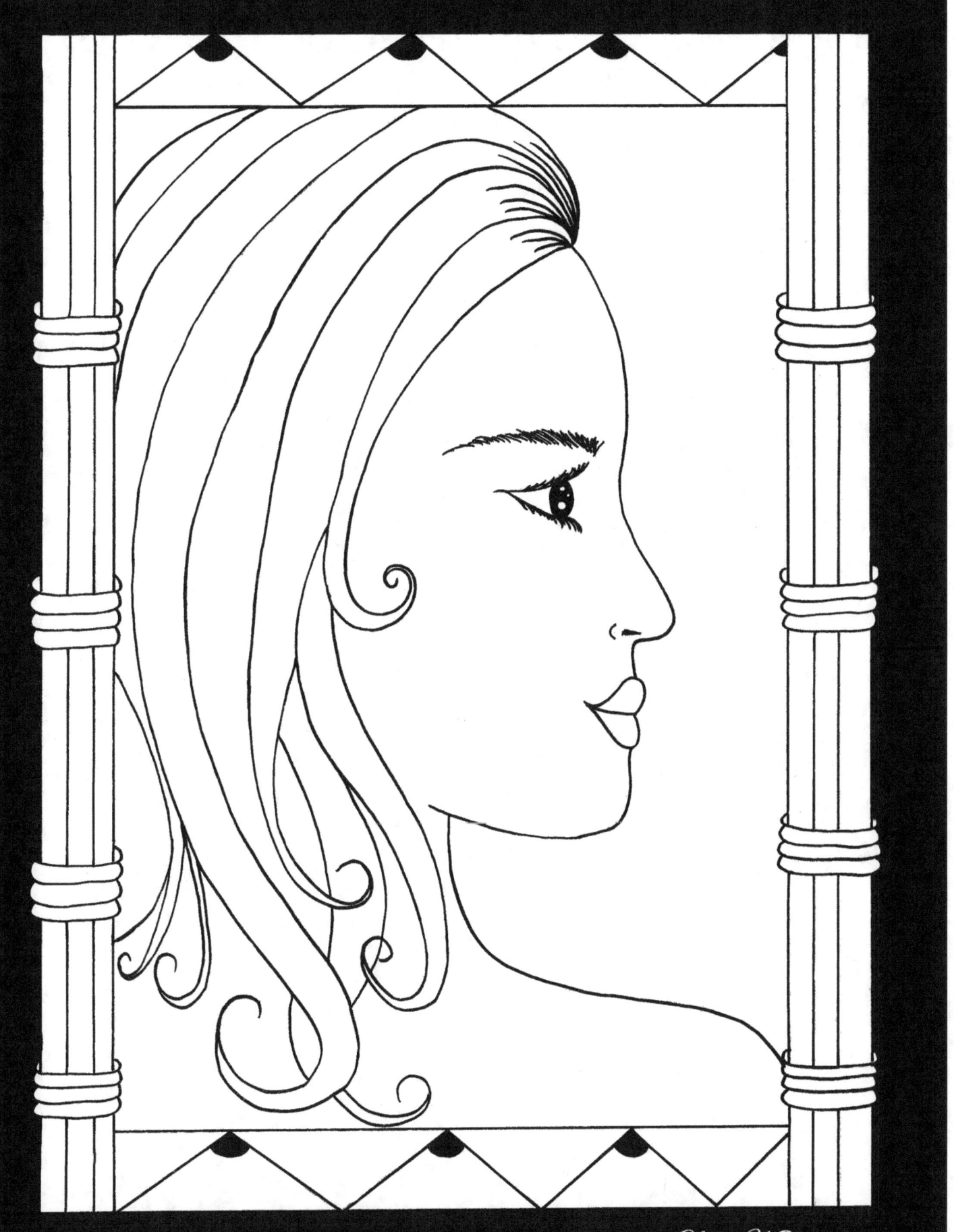

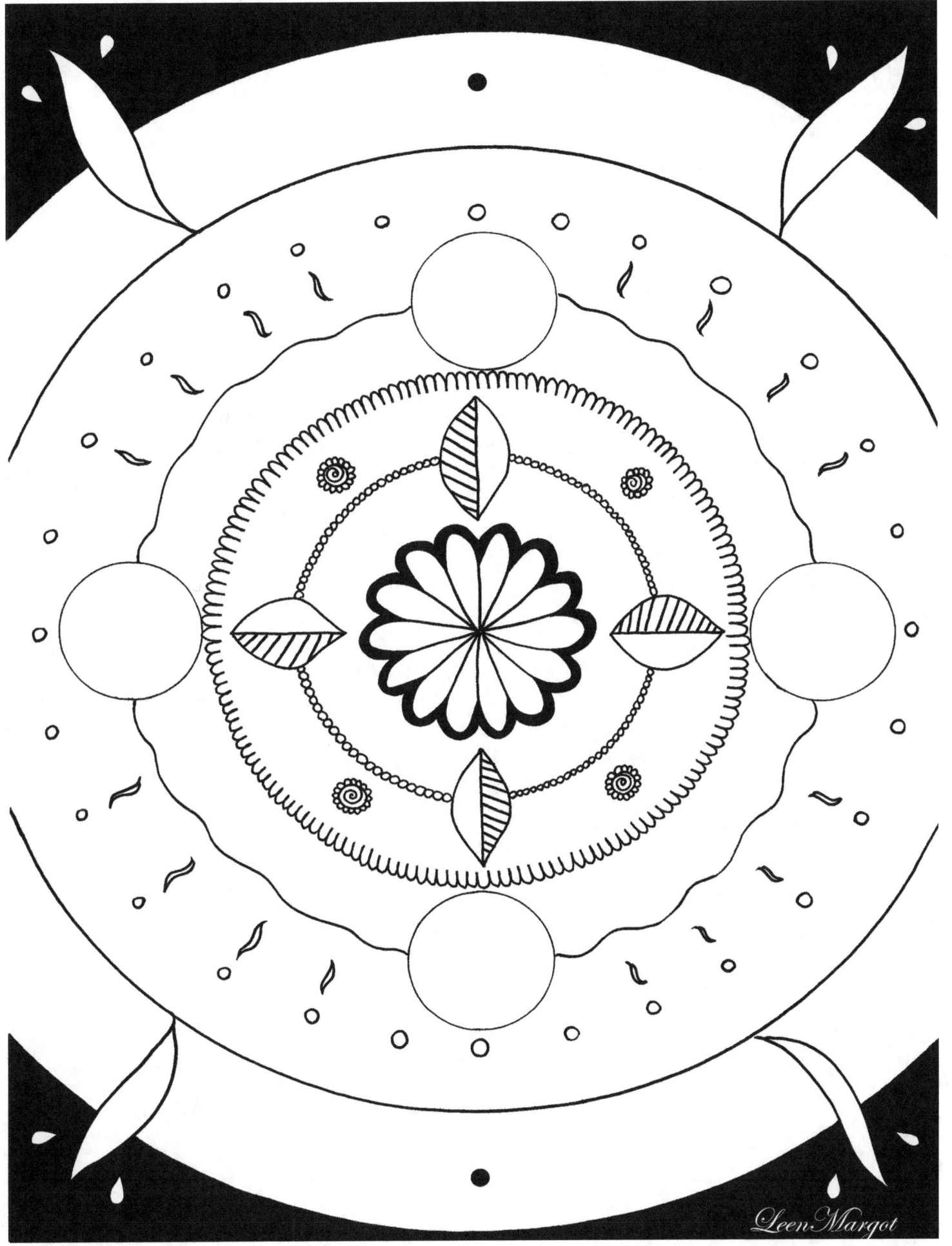

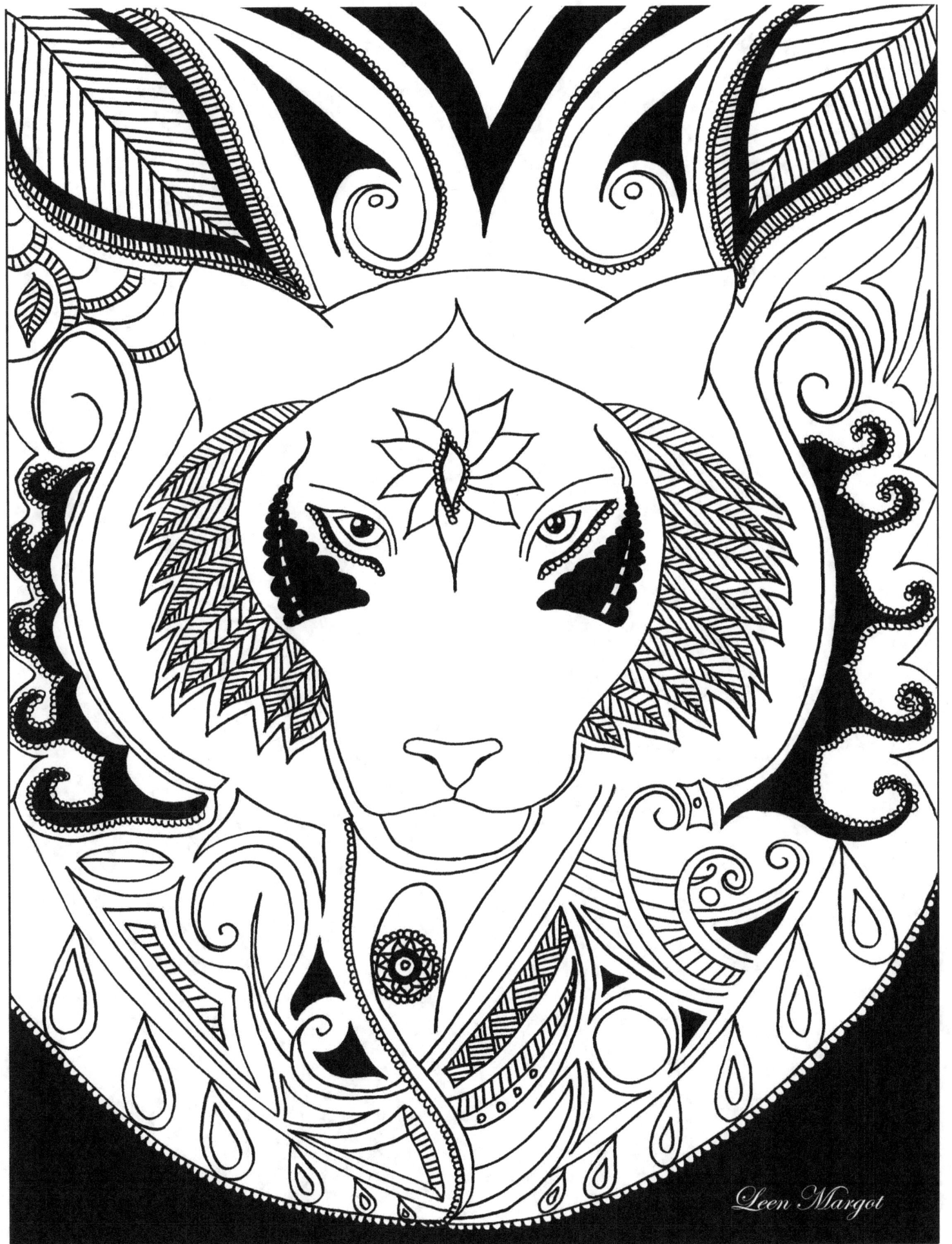

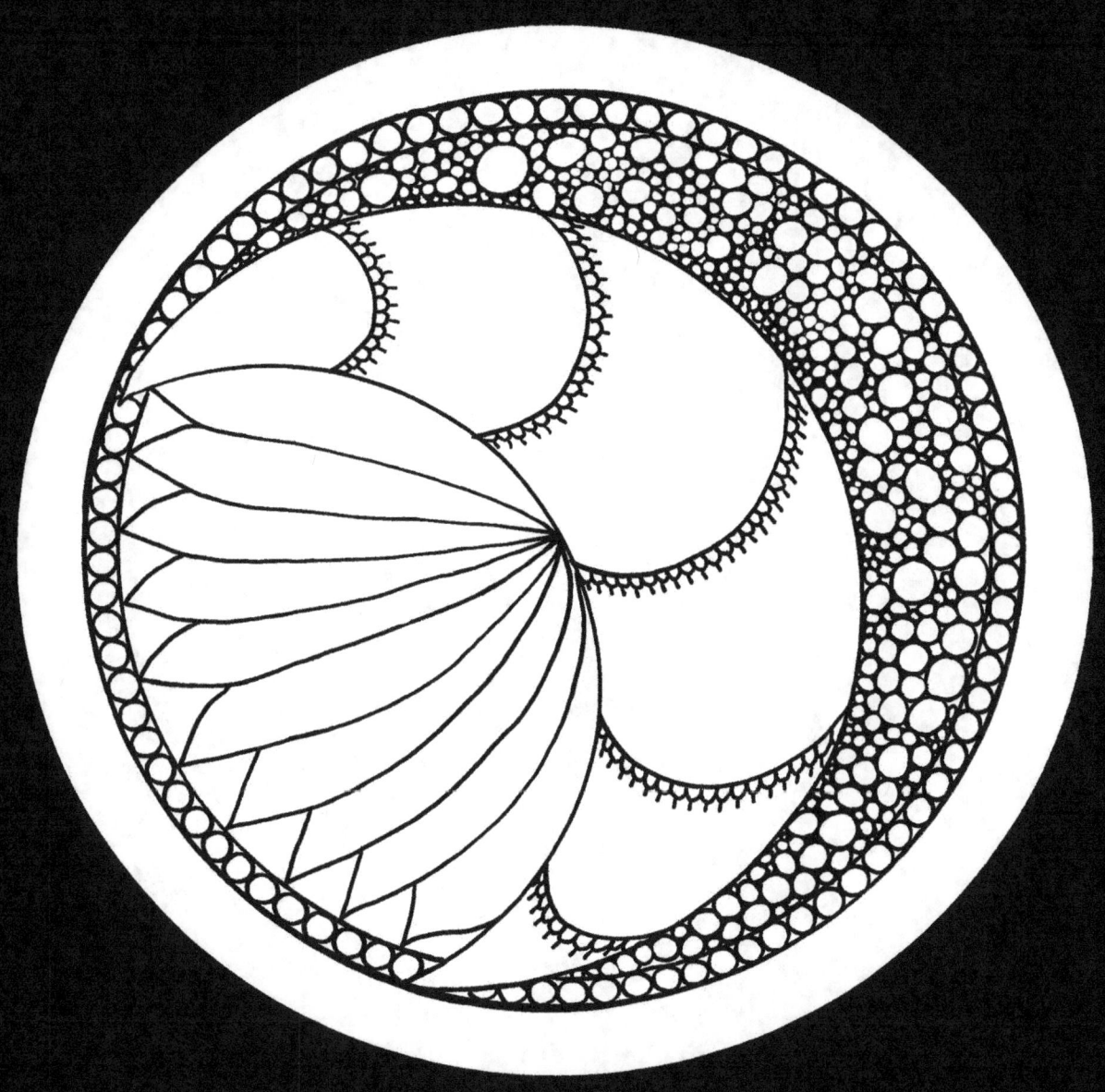

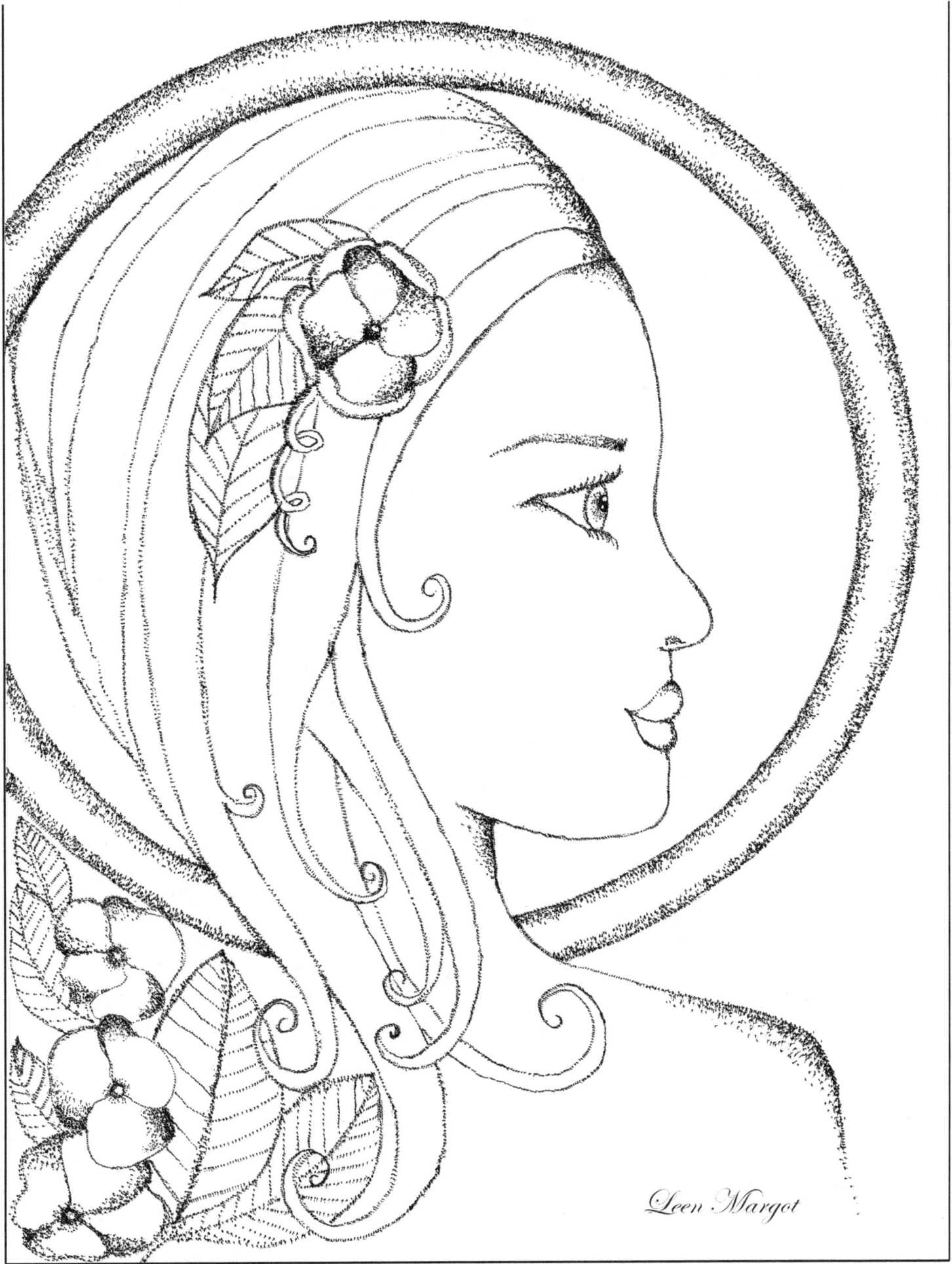

Chapter 7
Casey "Keyesay" Gilmore
USA

Facebook : keyesaysfineart
Etsy shop : KeyesaysVisualArt

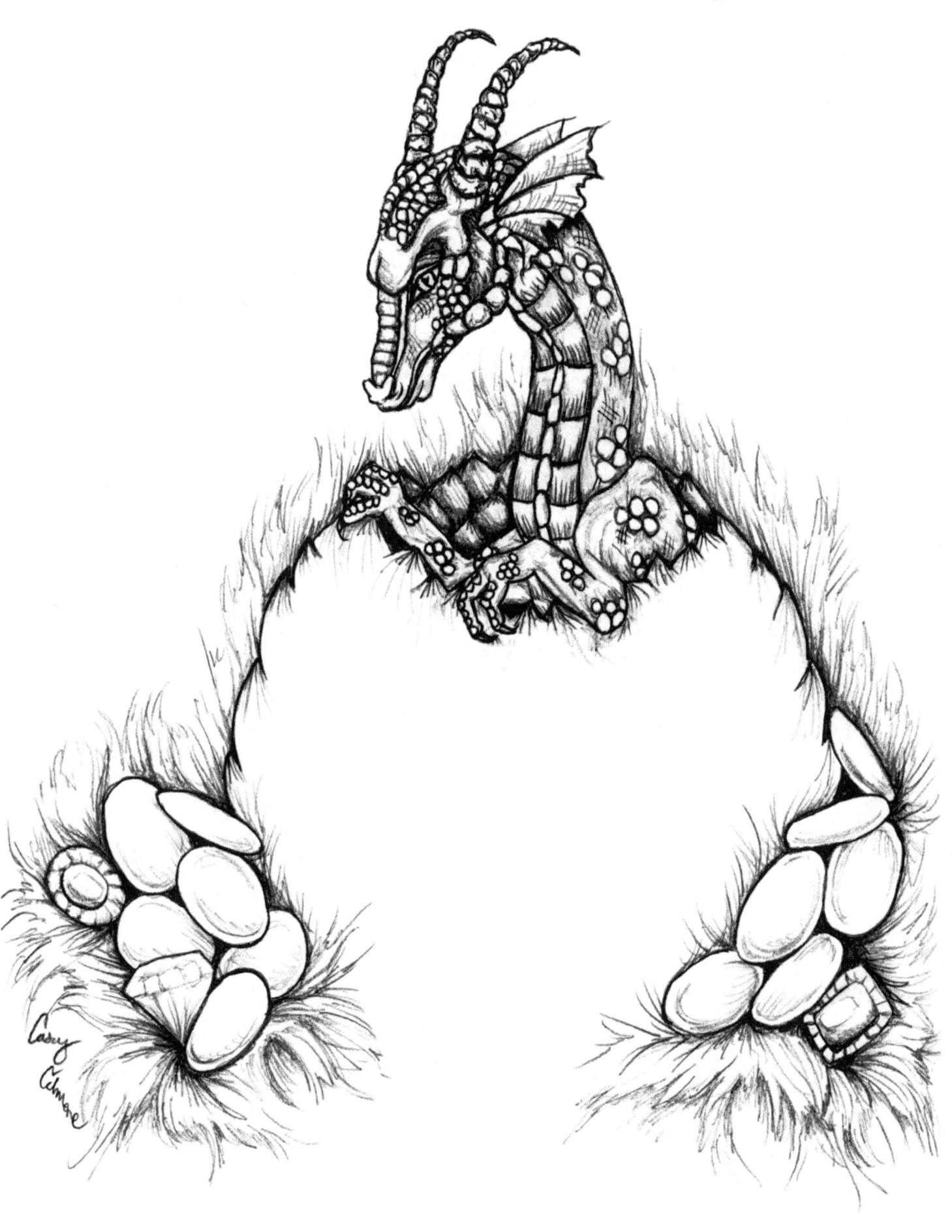

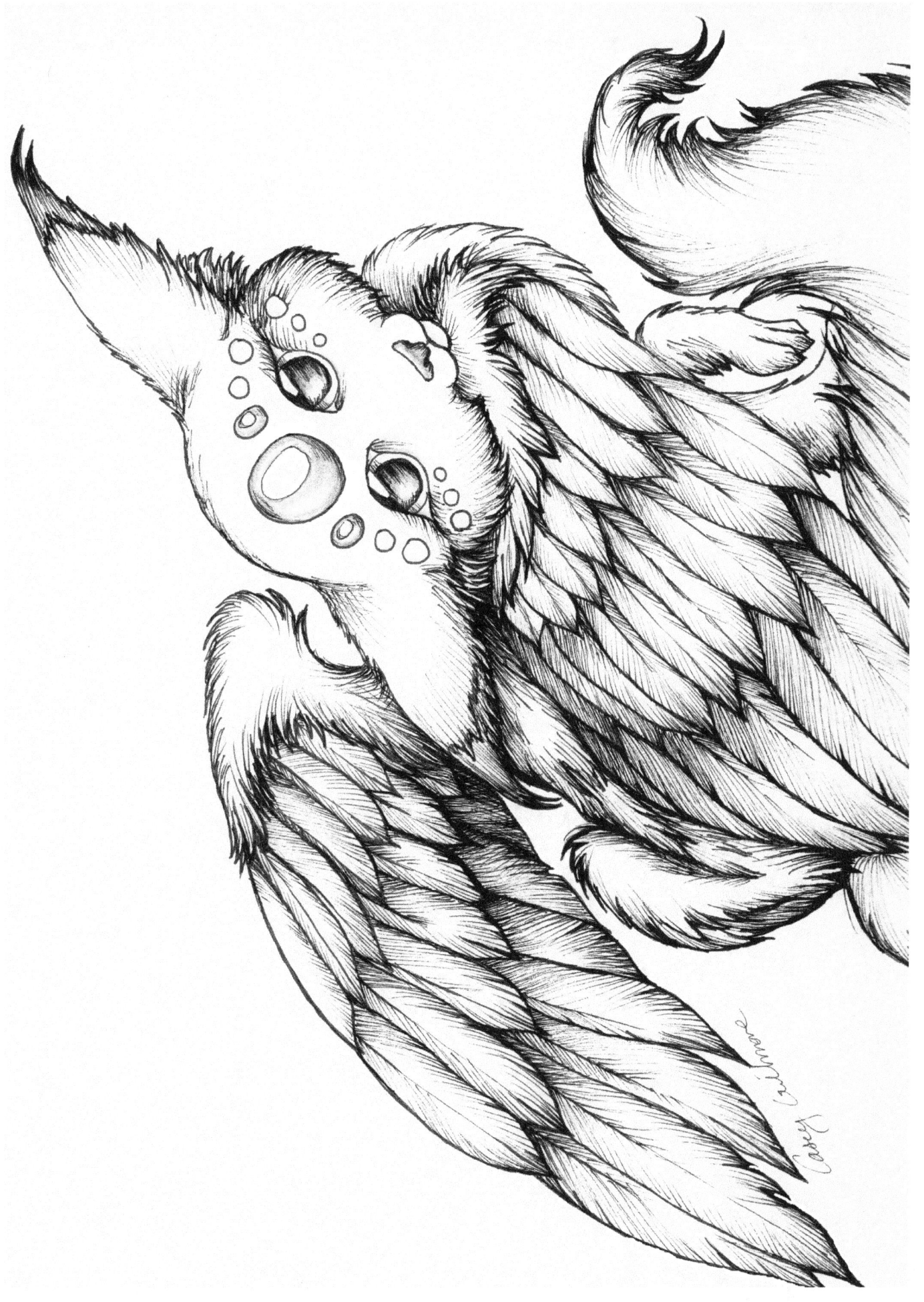

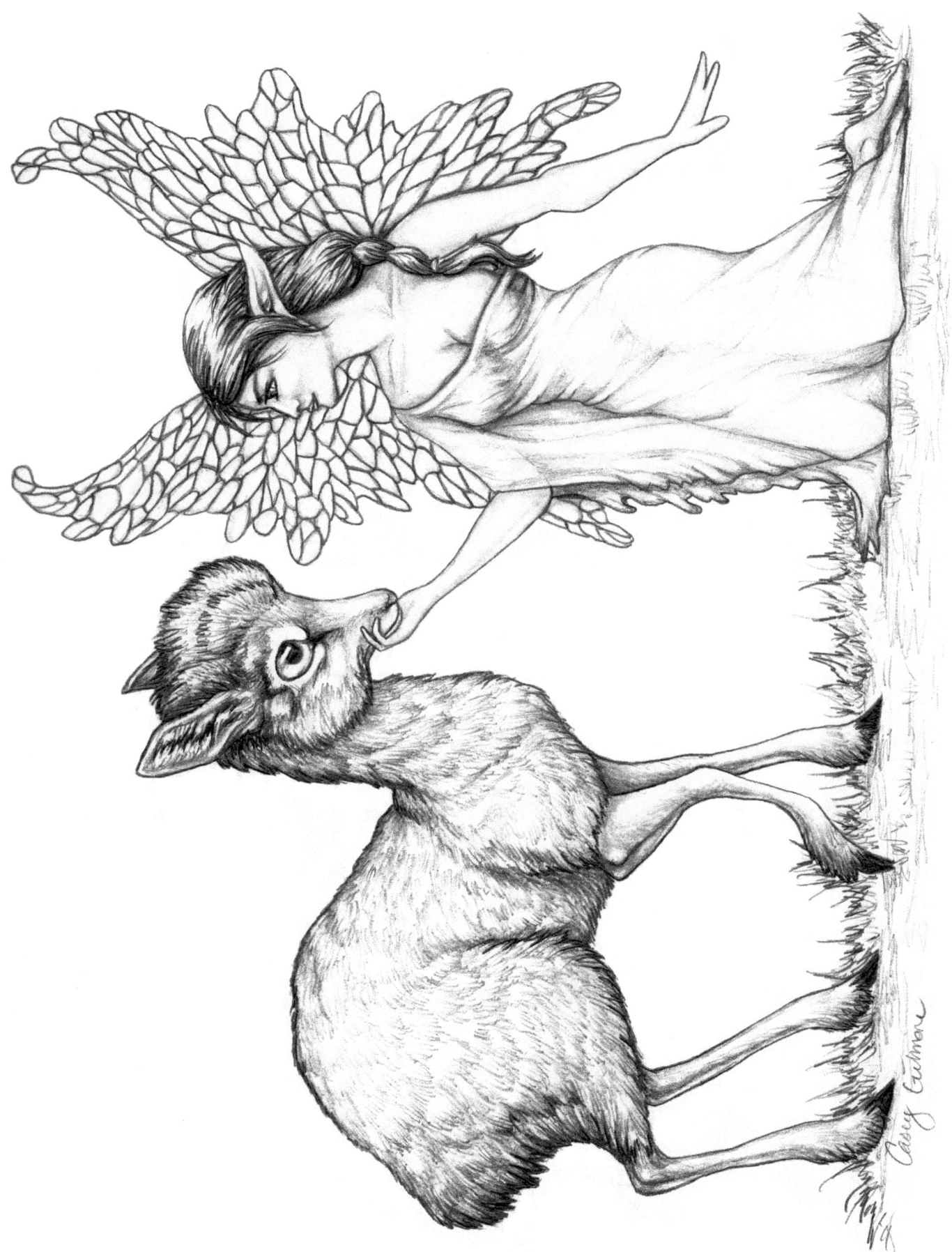

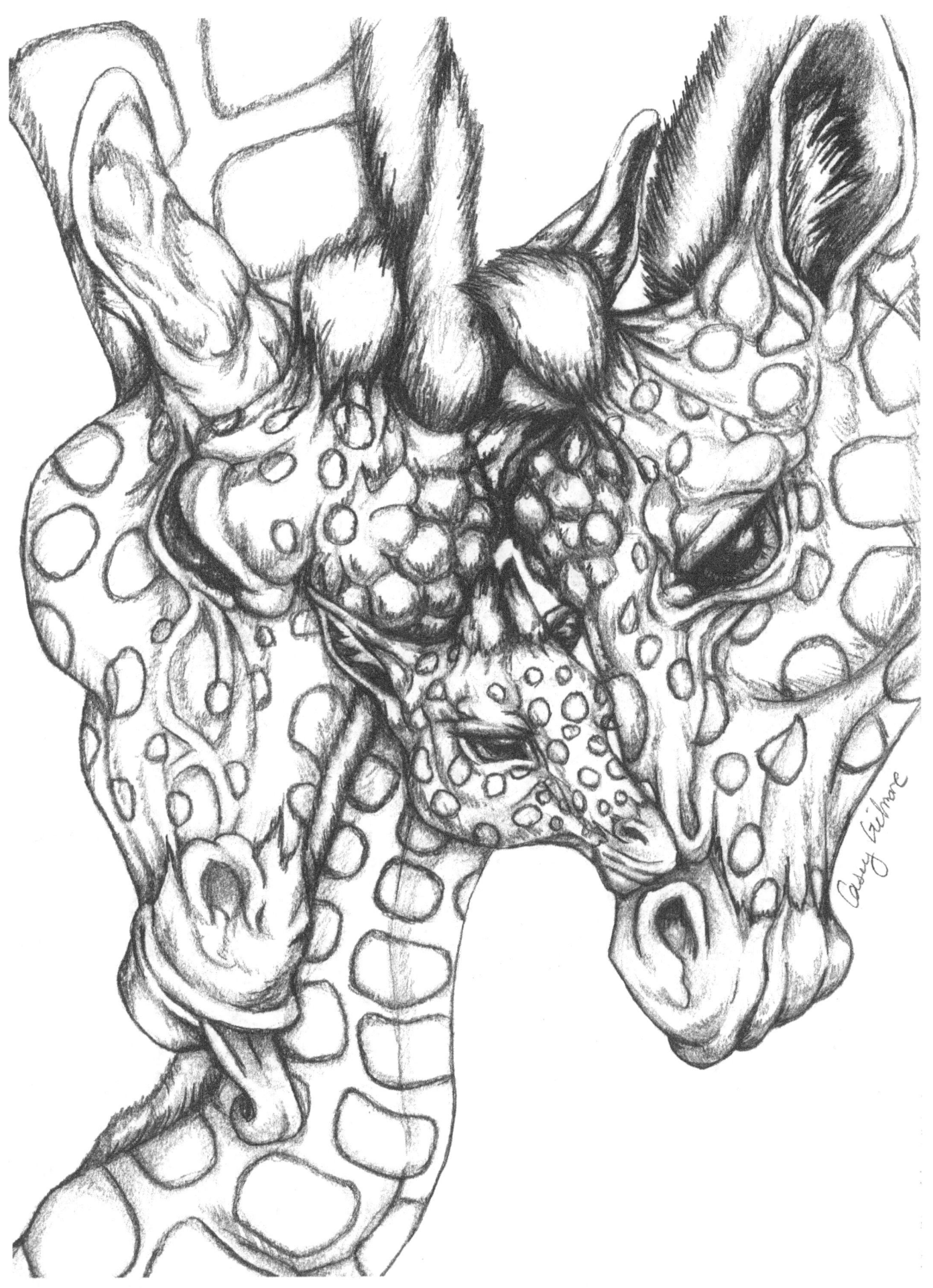

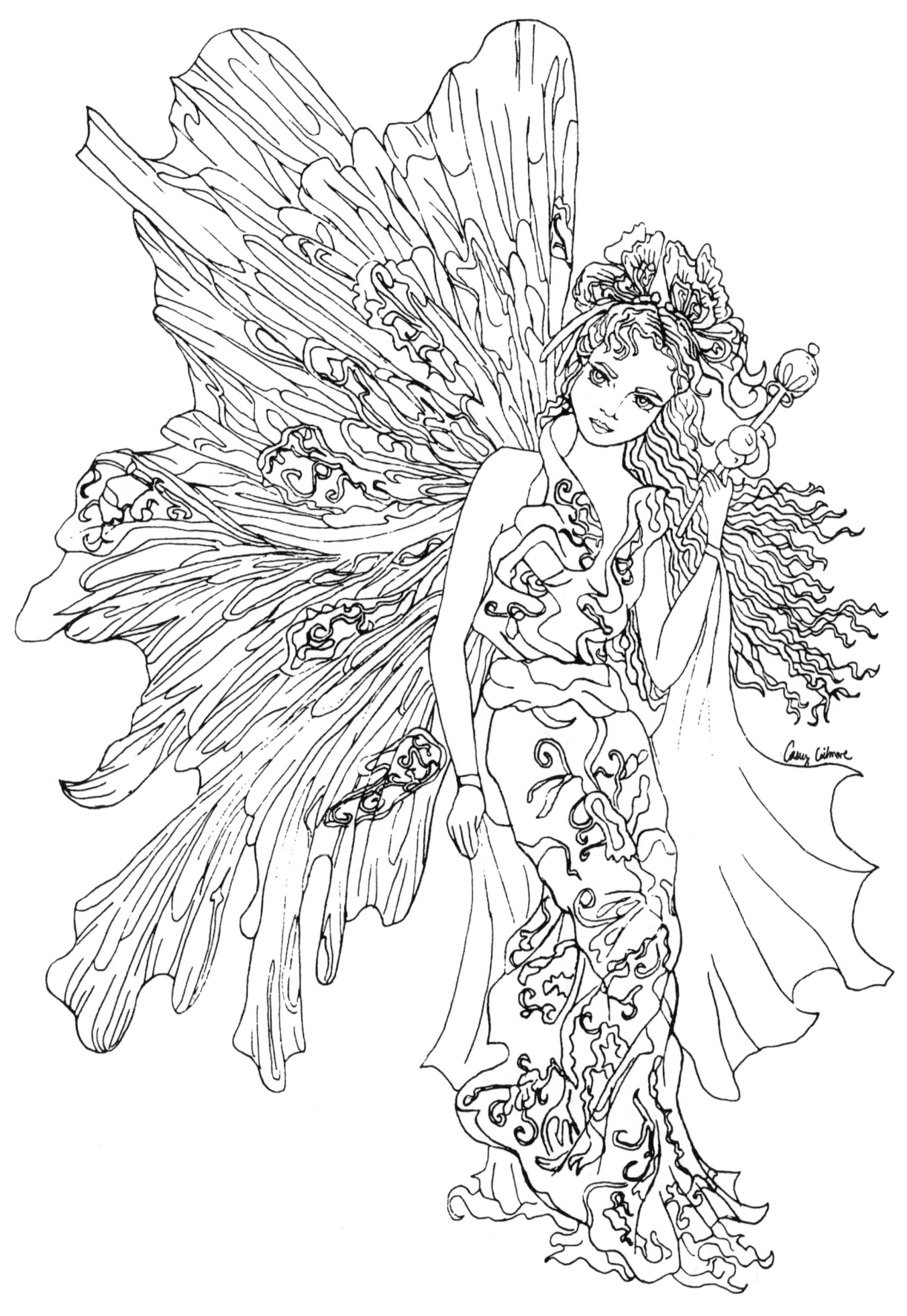

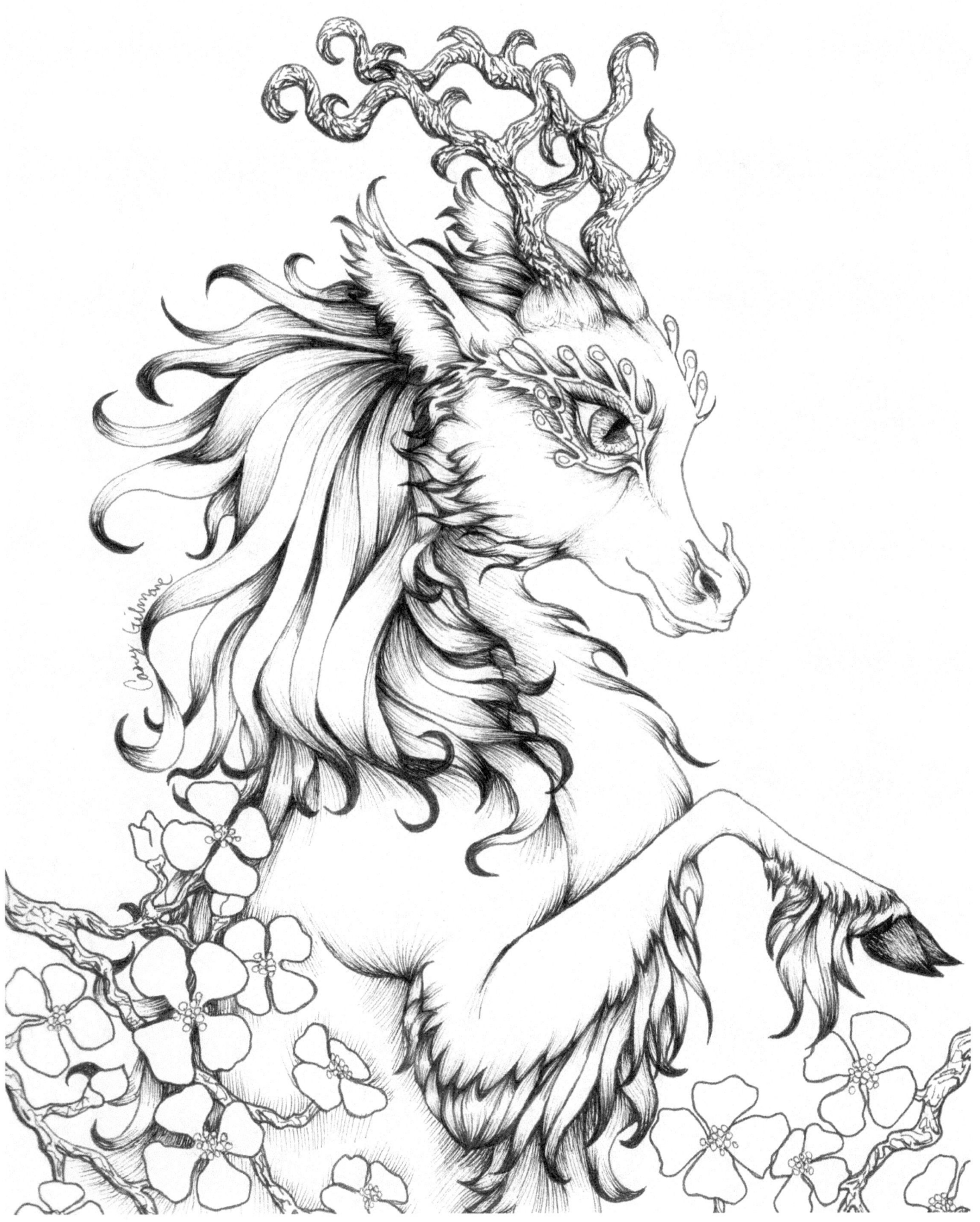

Chapter 8
Fafahé
France

Facebook : Fafahe-creations
https://www.youtube.com/channel/UCKLs-zt2s5ZsIrFegLjHfoA

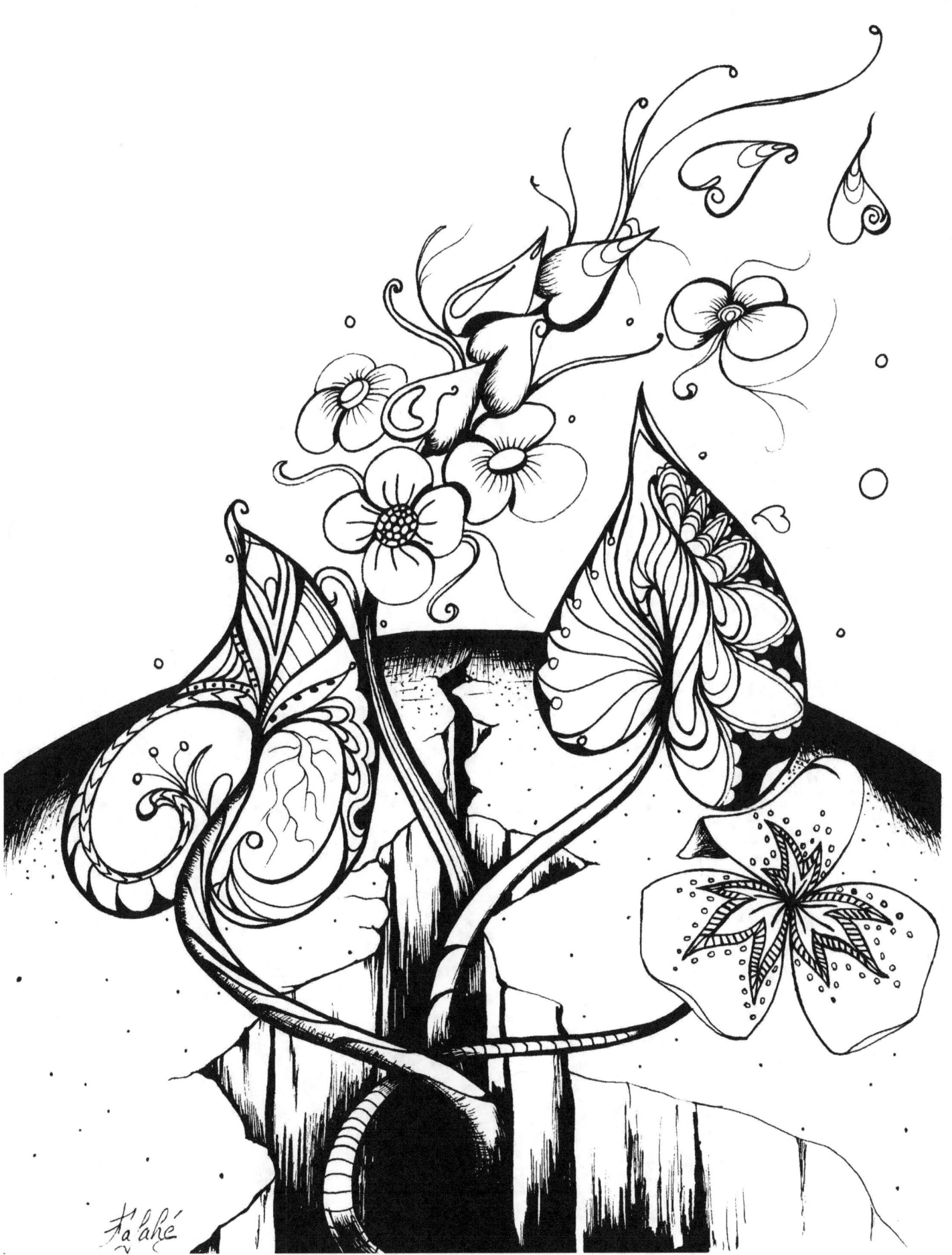

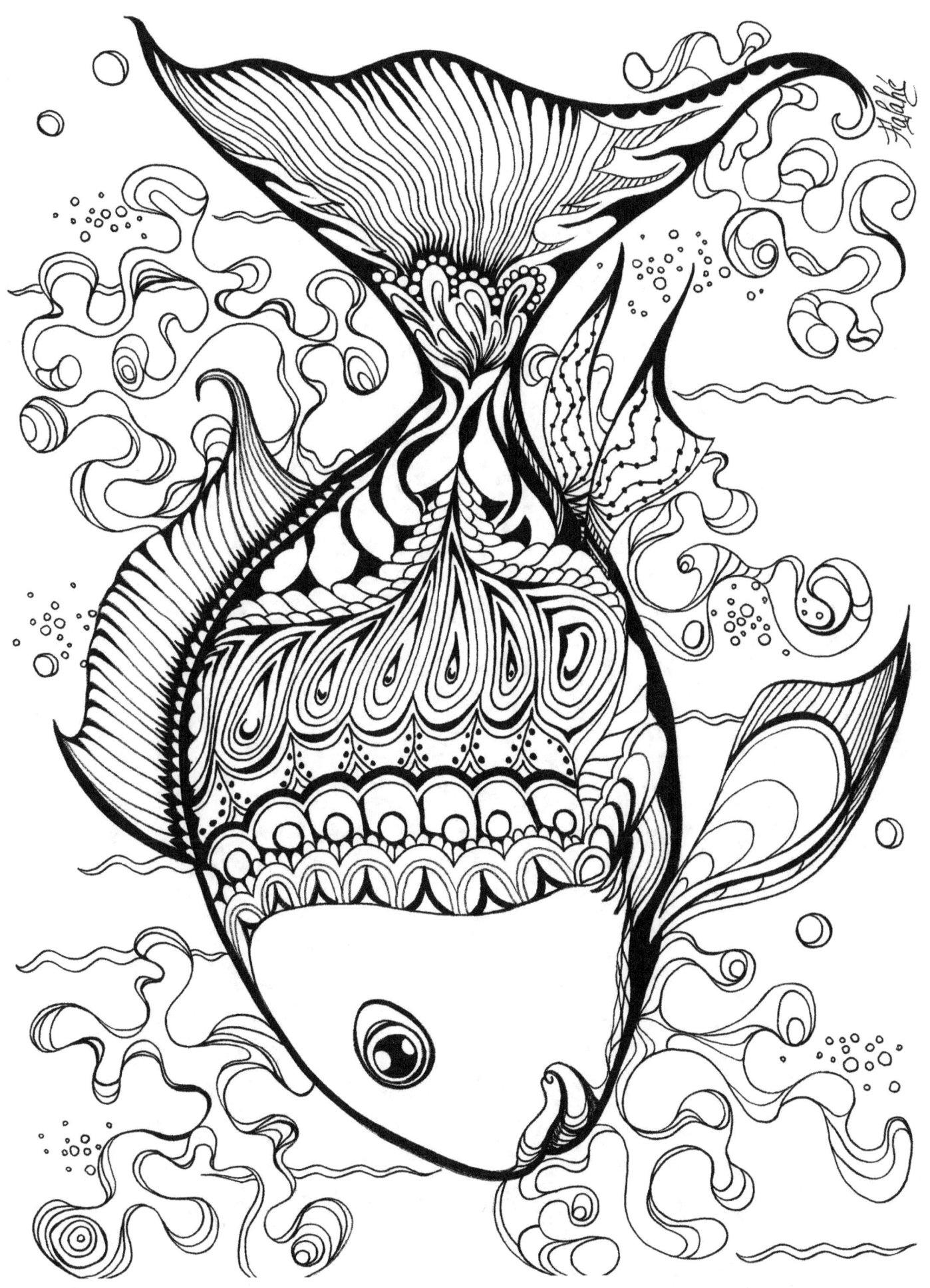

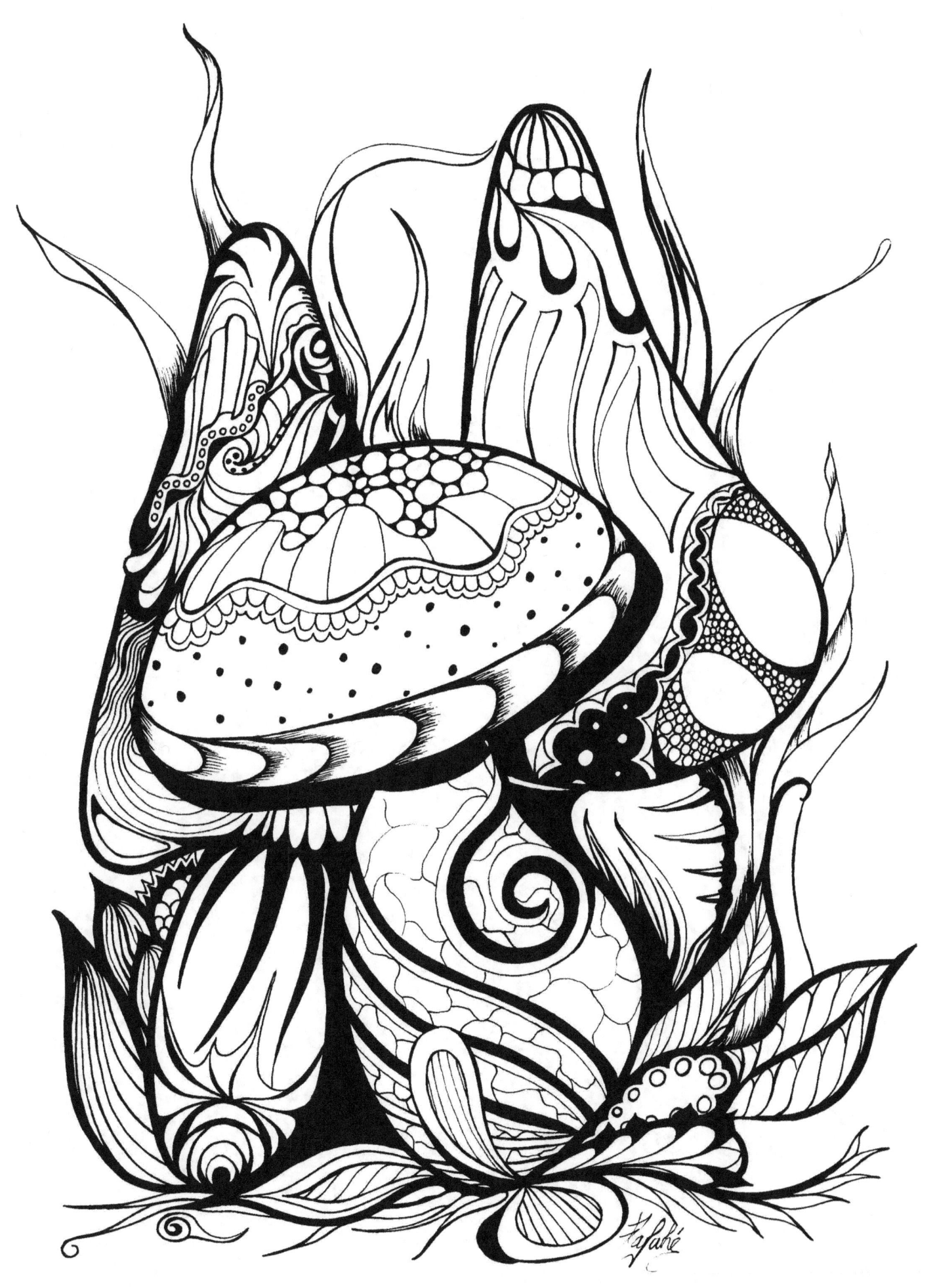

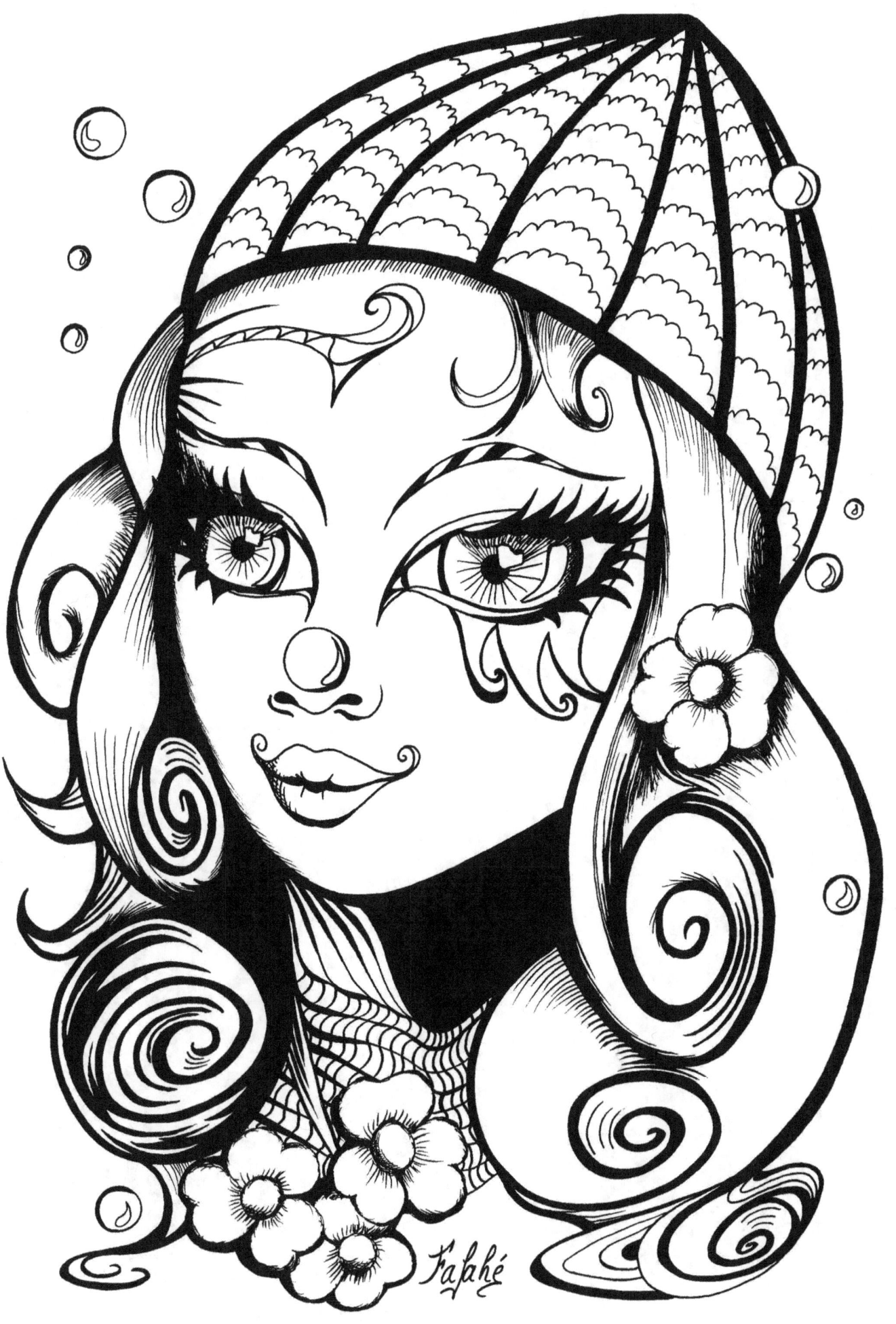

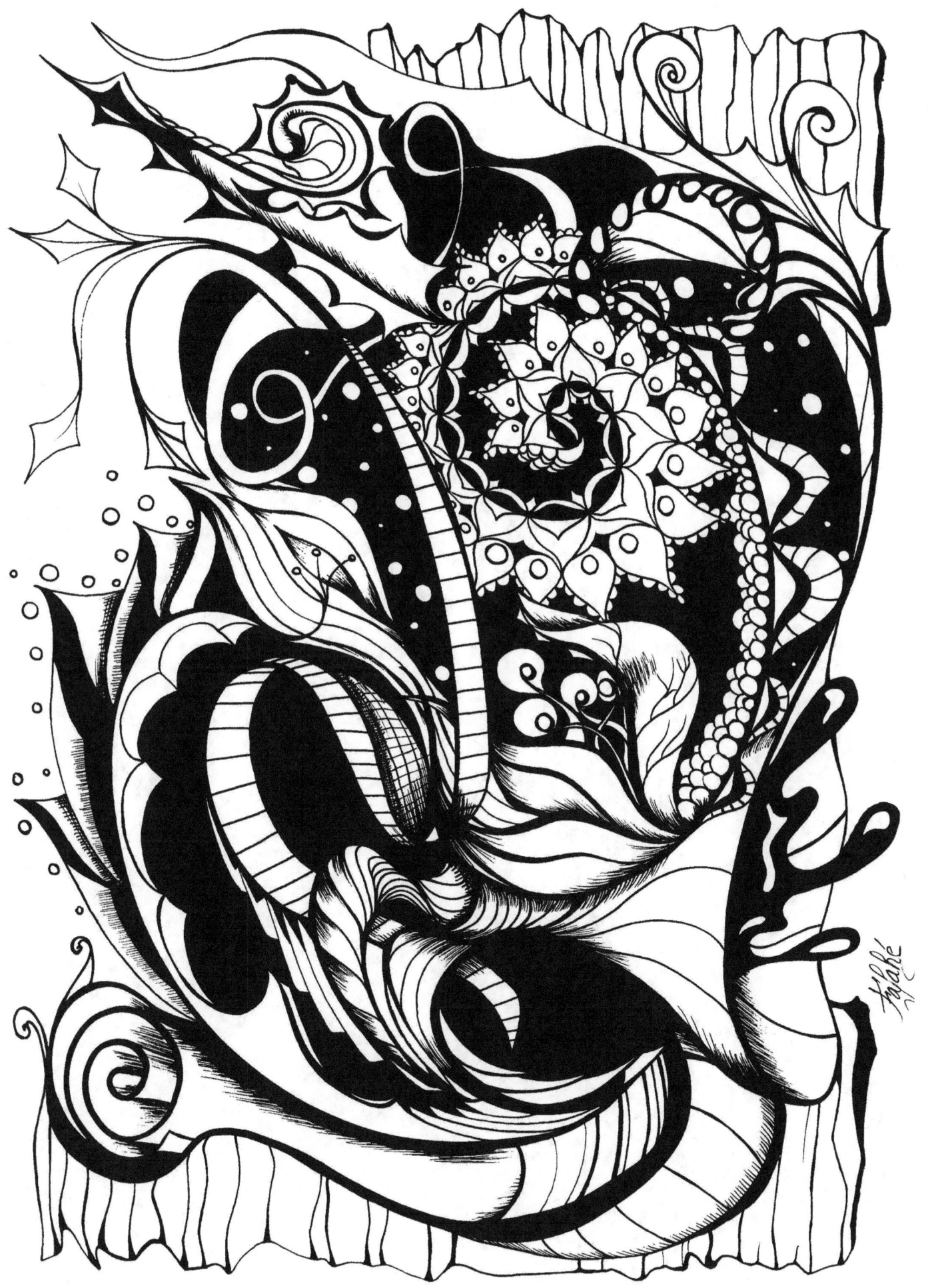

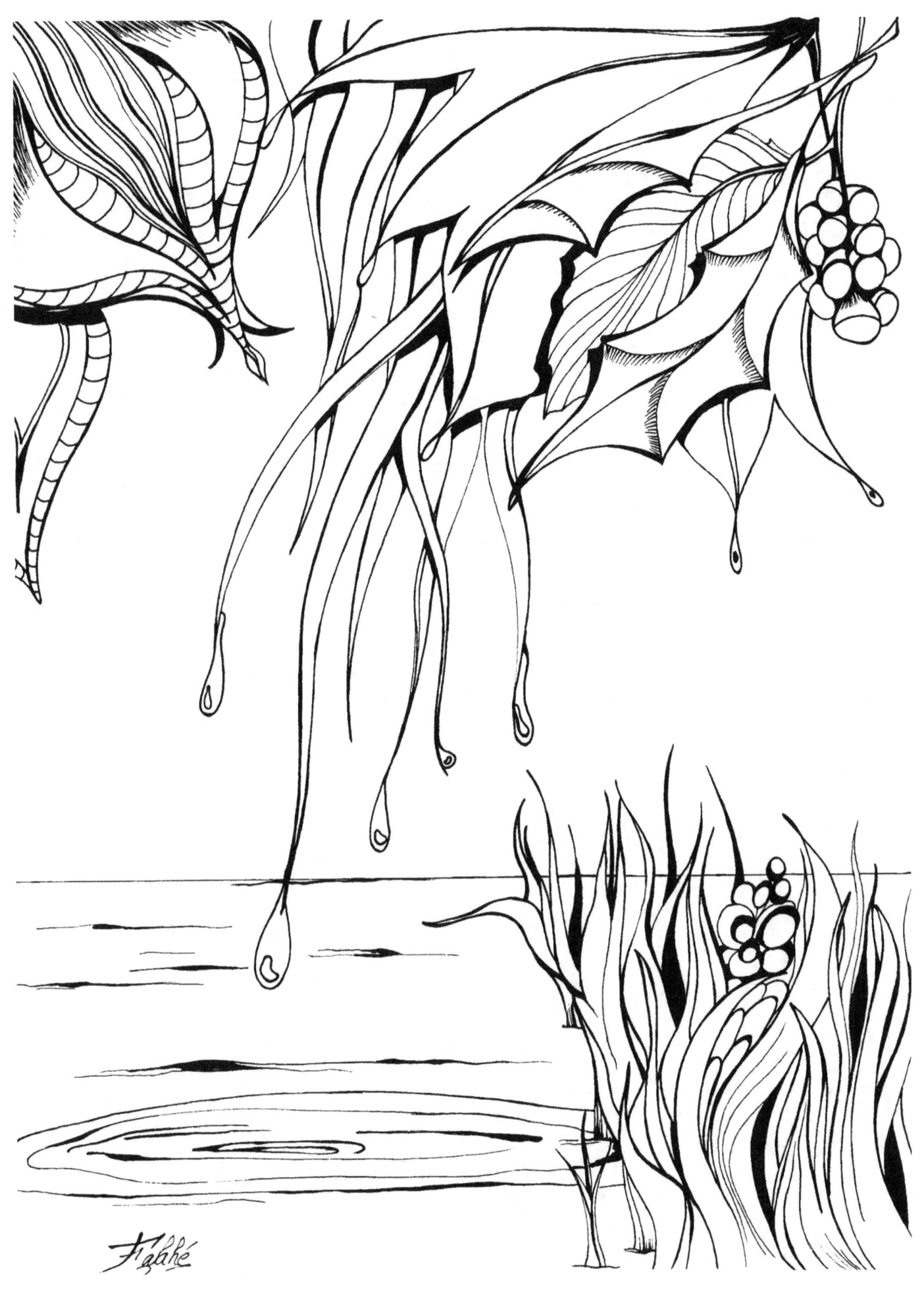

Chapter 9
Iben Lykke Højholdt
Denmark

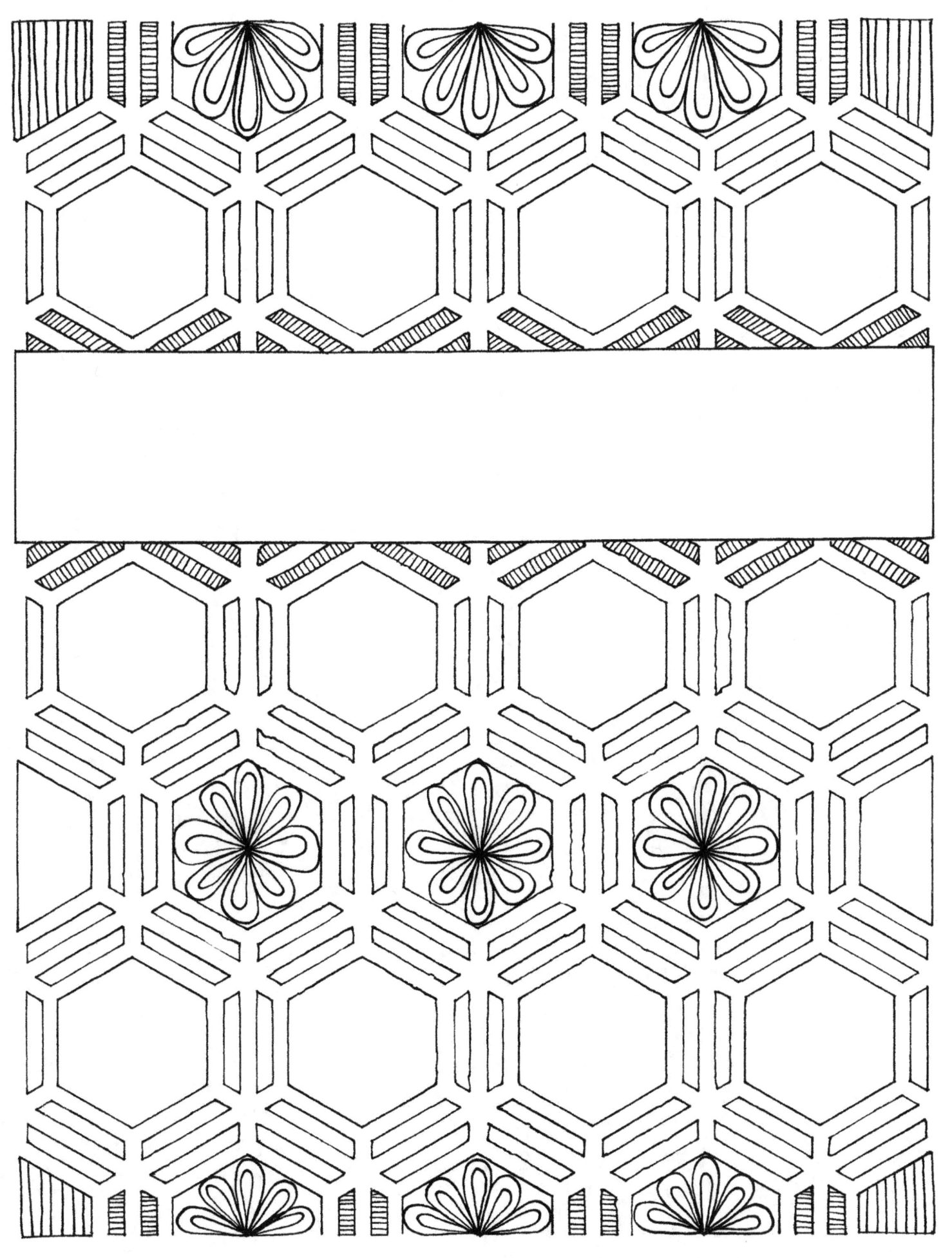

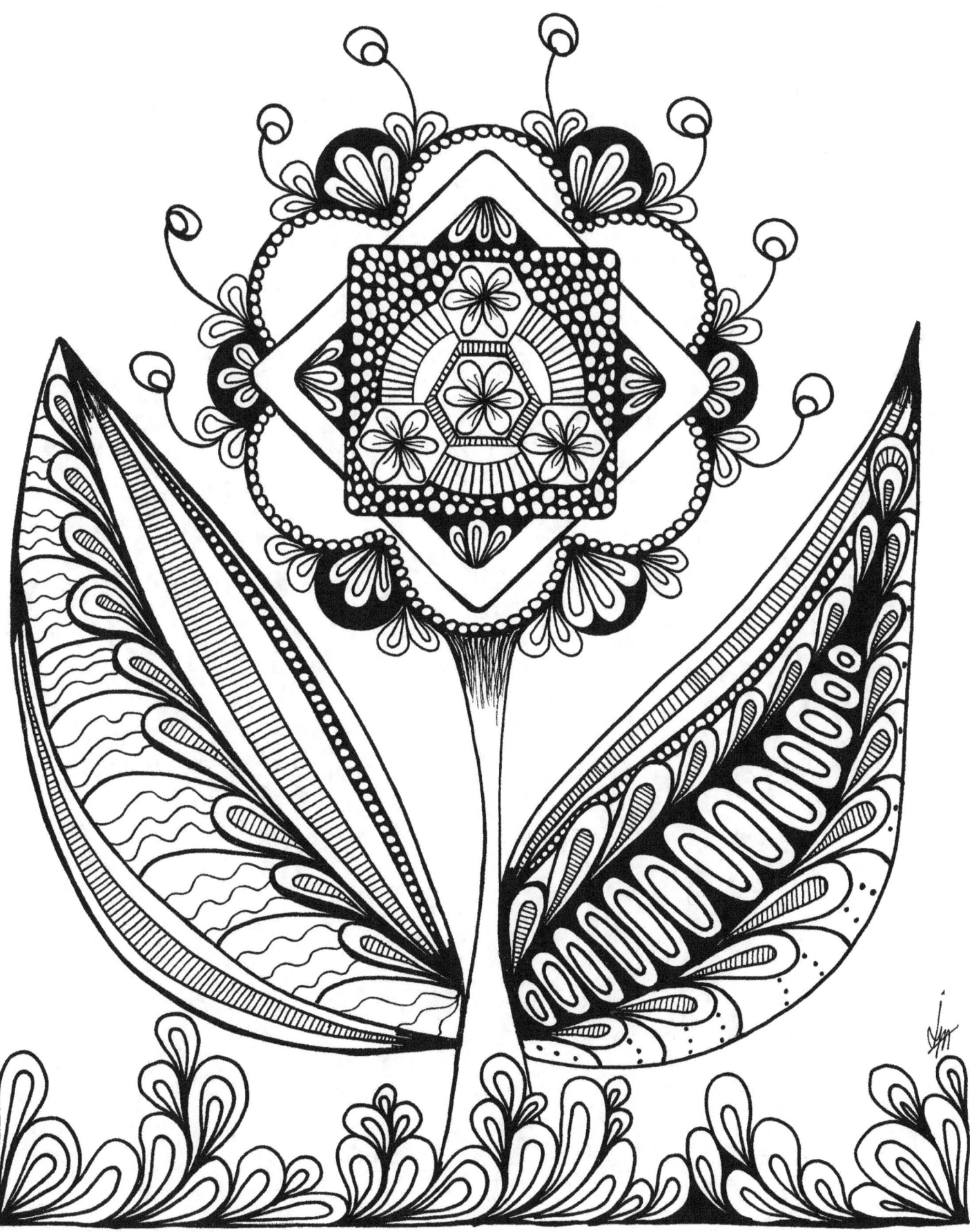

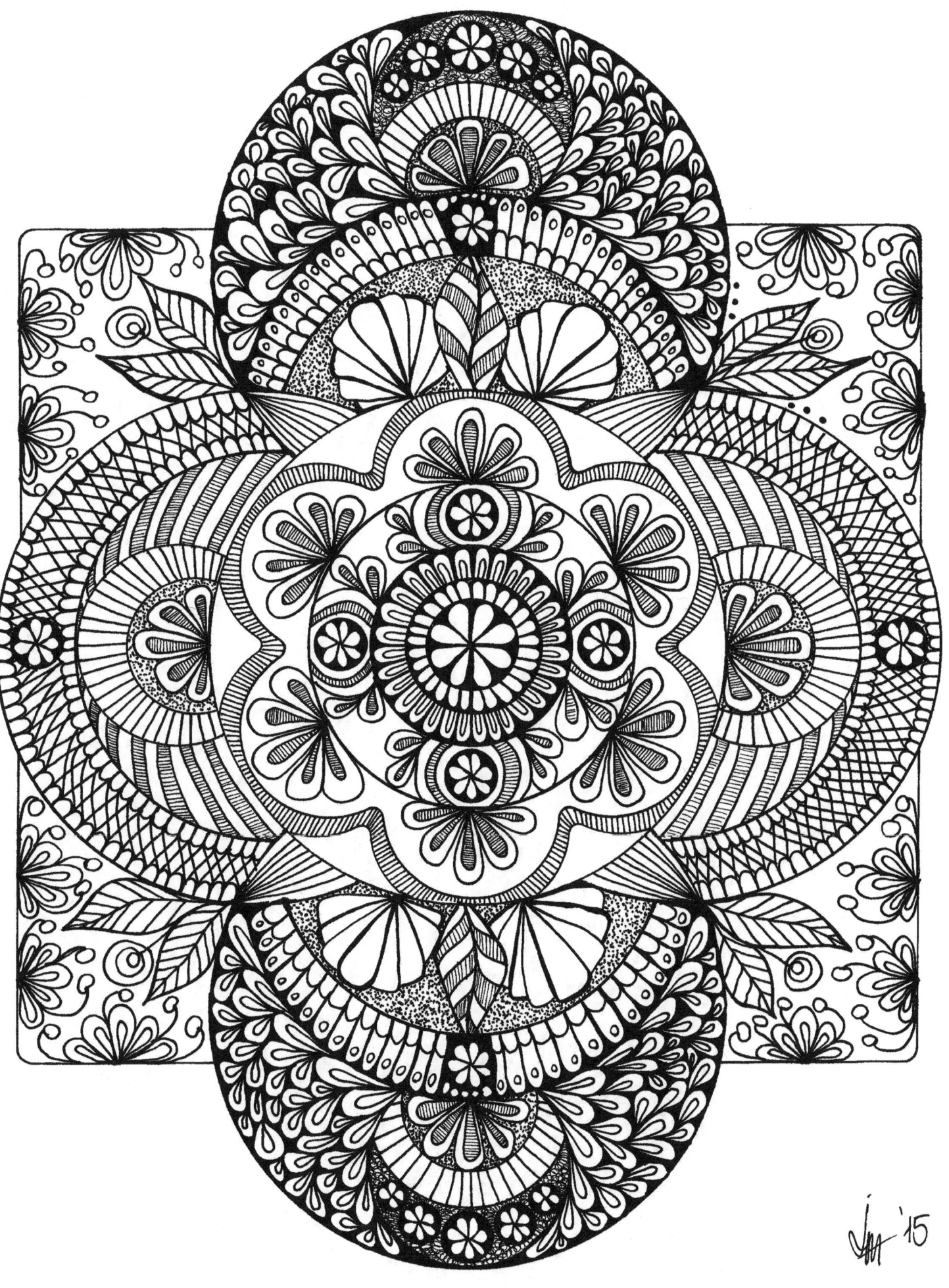

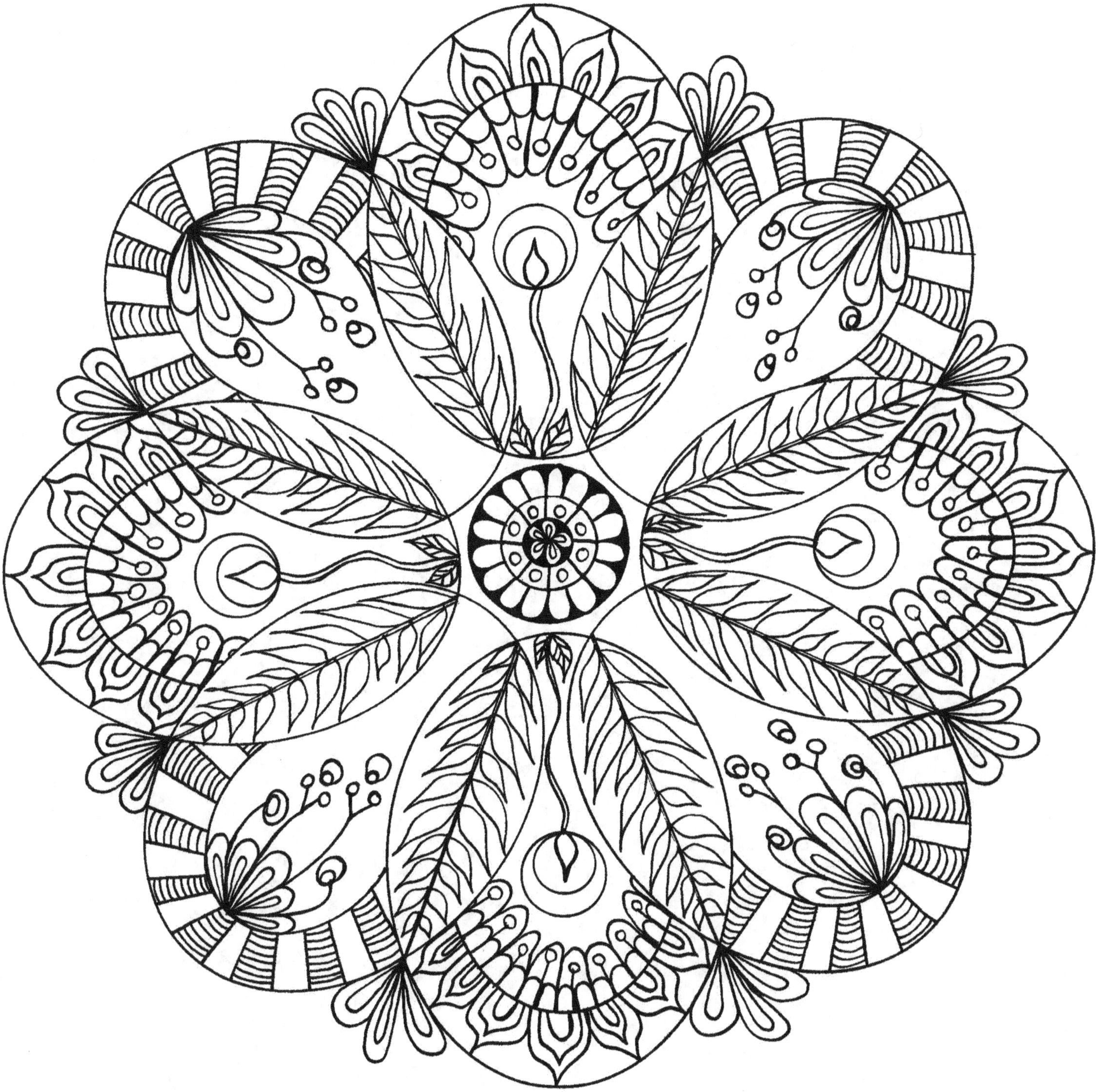

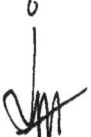

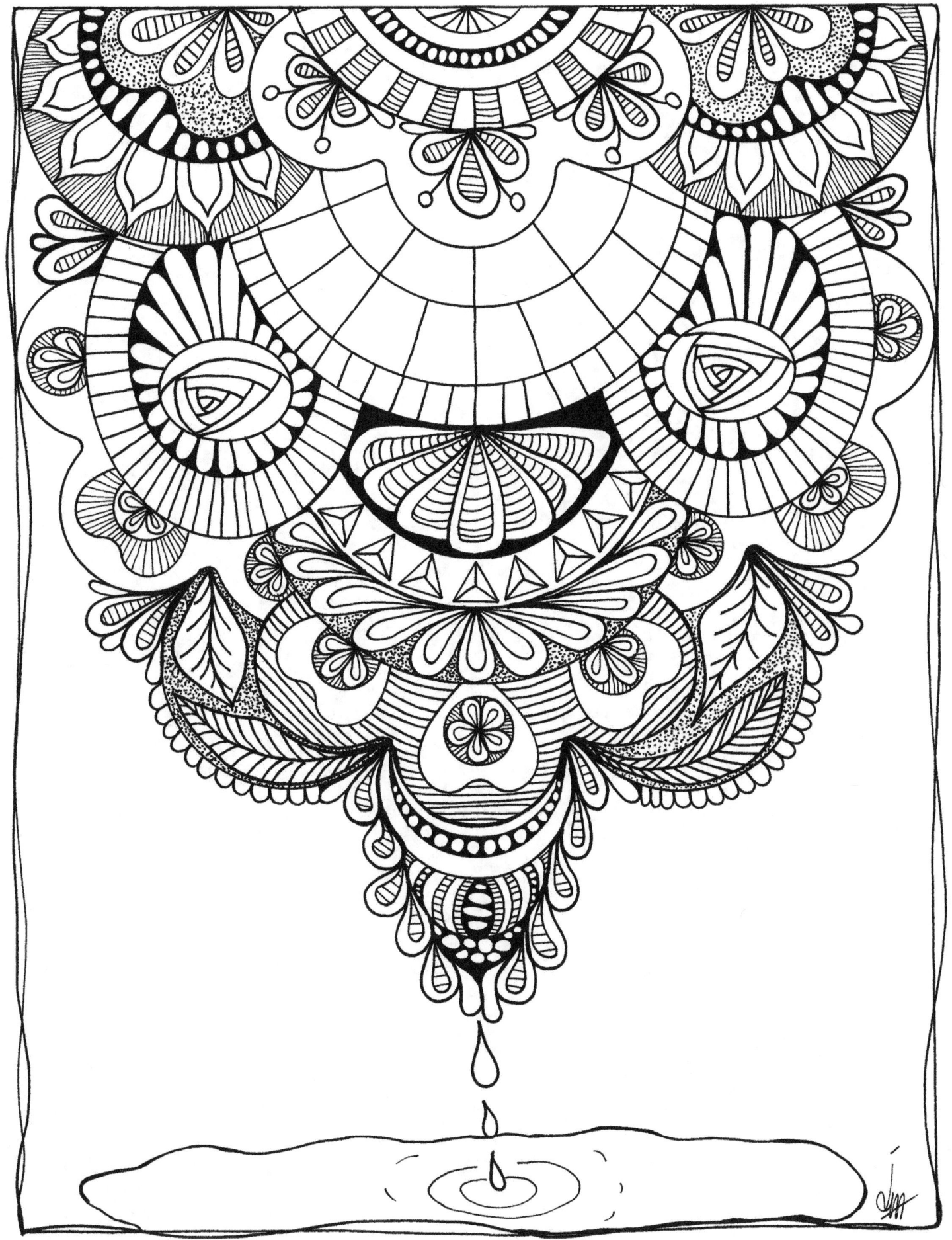

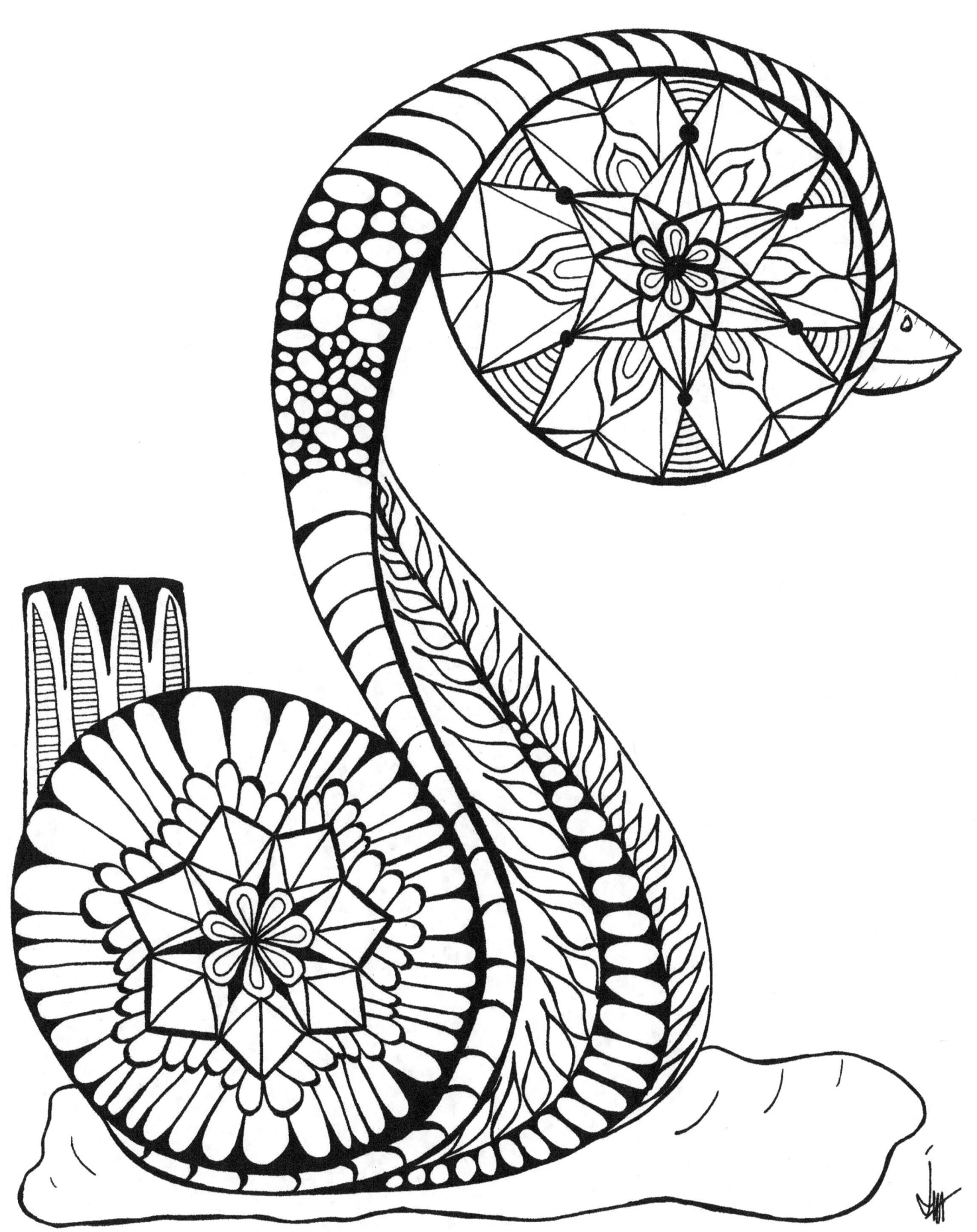

Chapter 10
Neeti Goswami
Canada

www.artbyneeti.ca

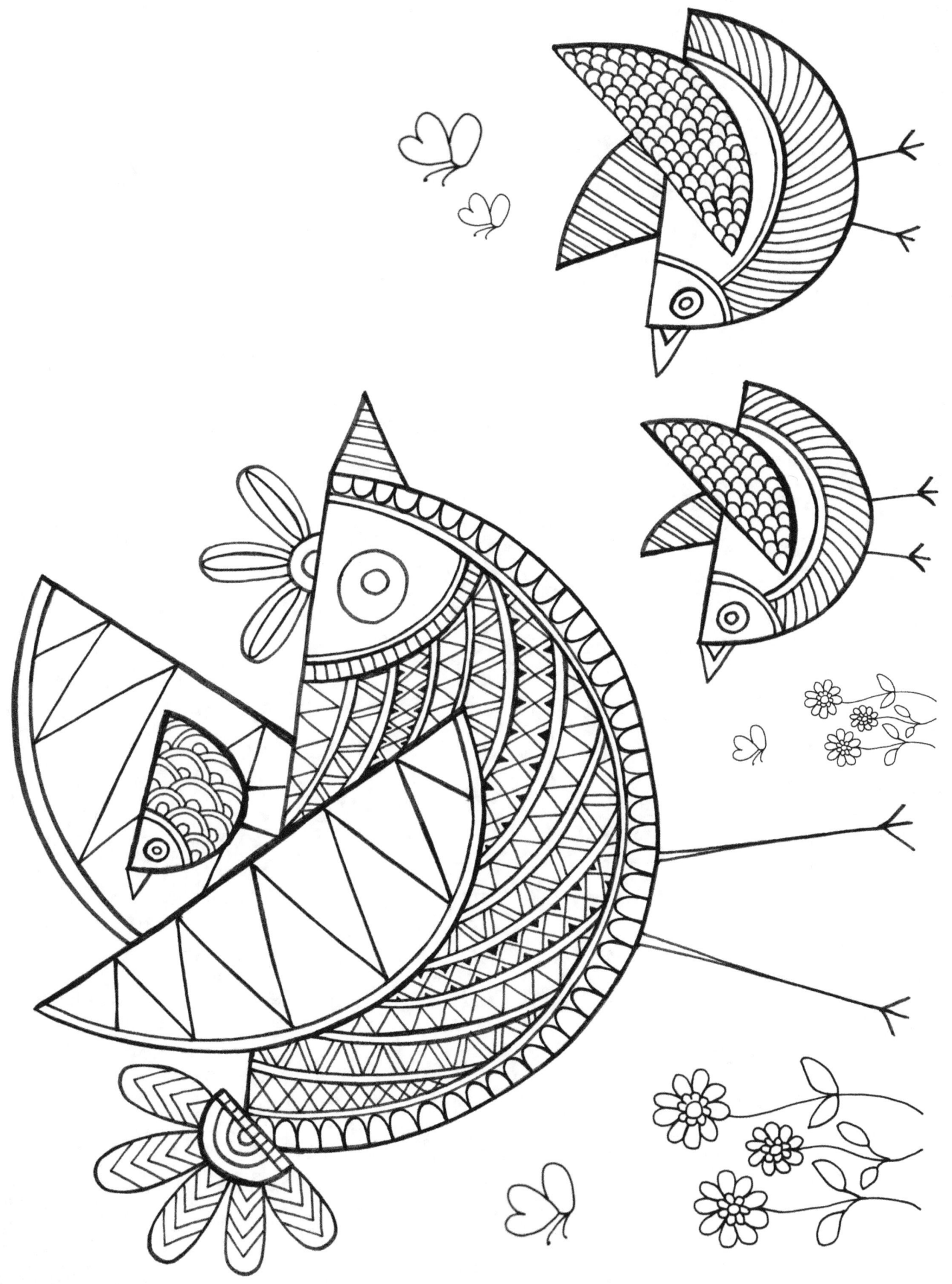

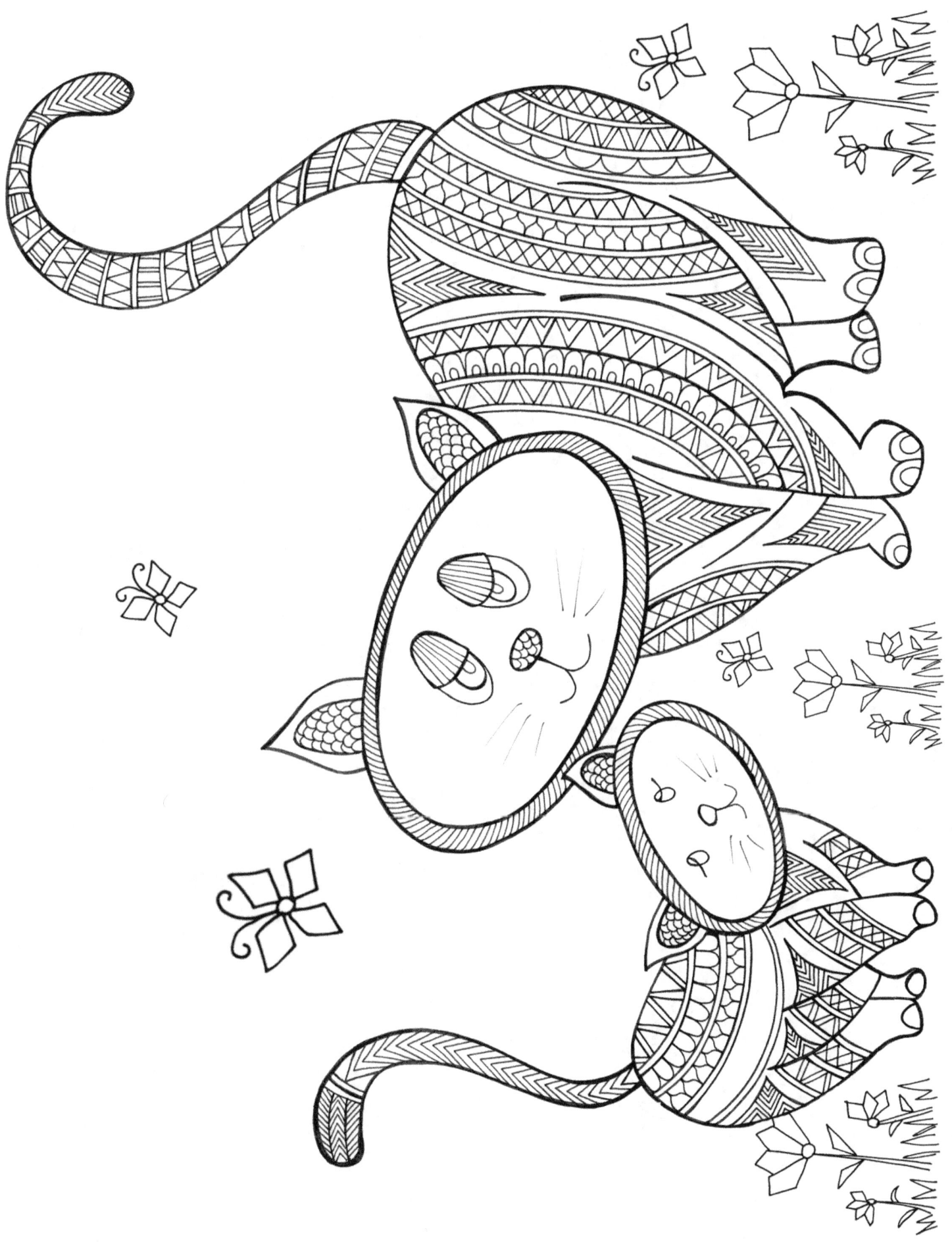

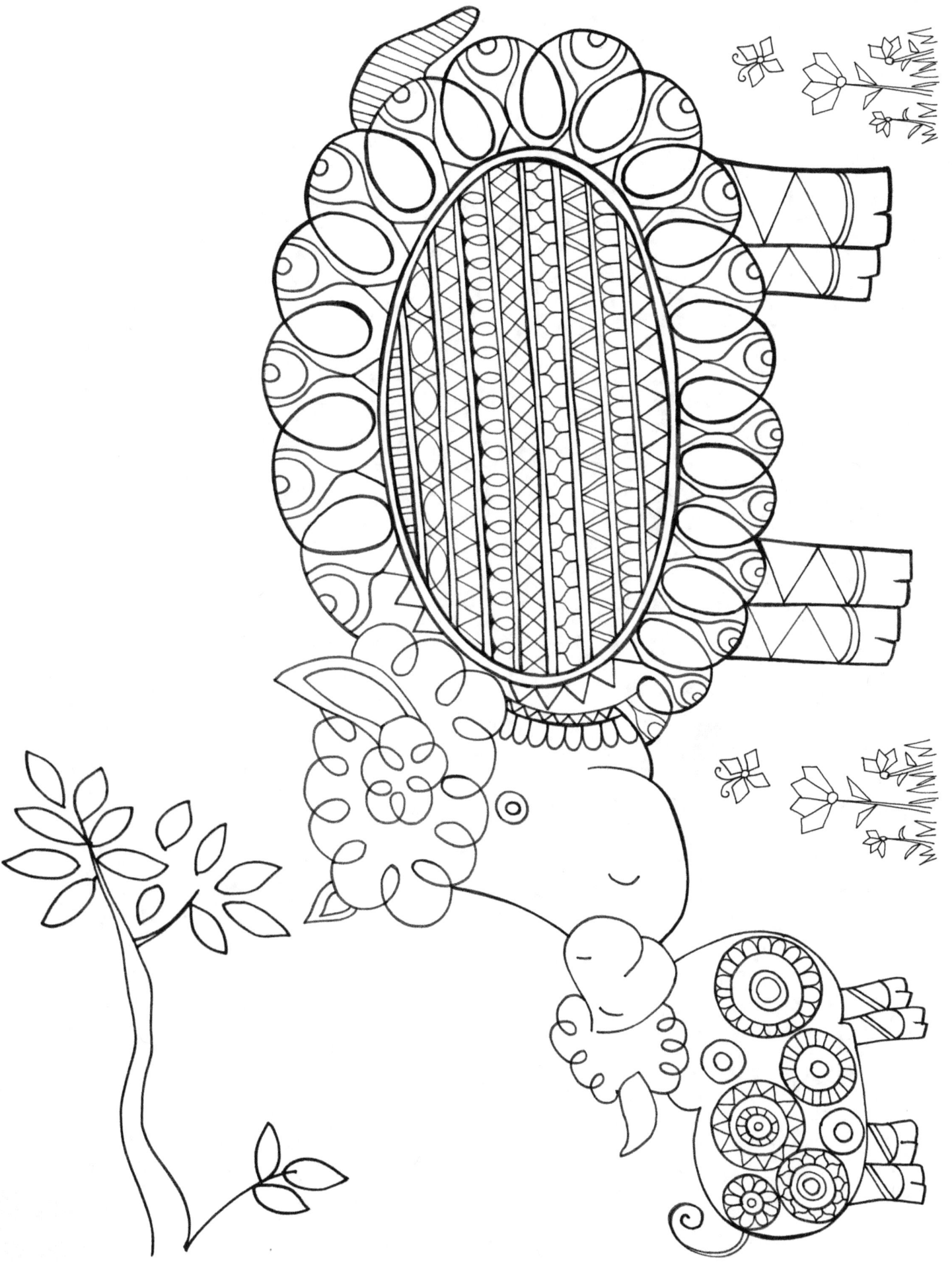

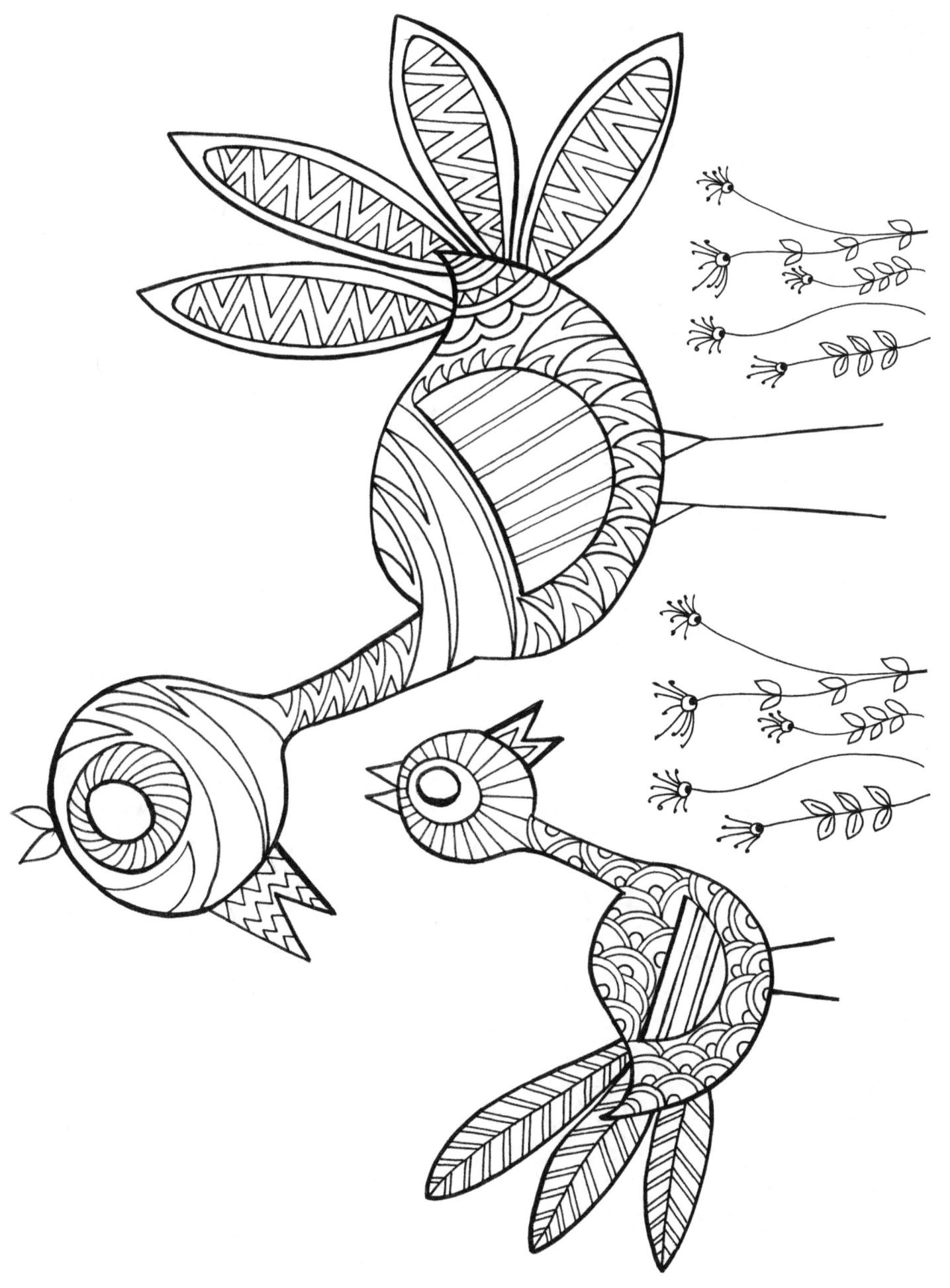

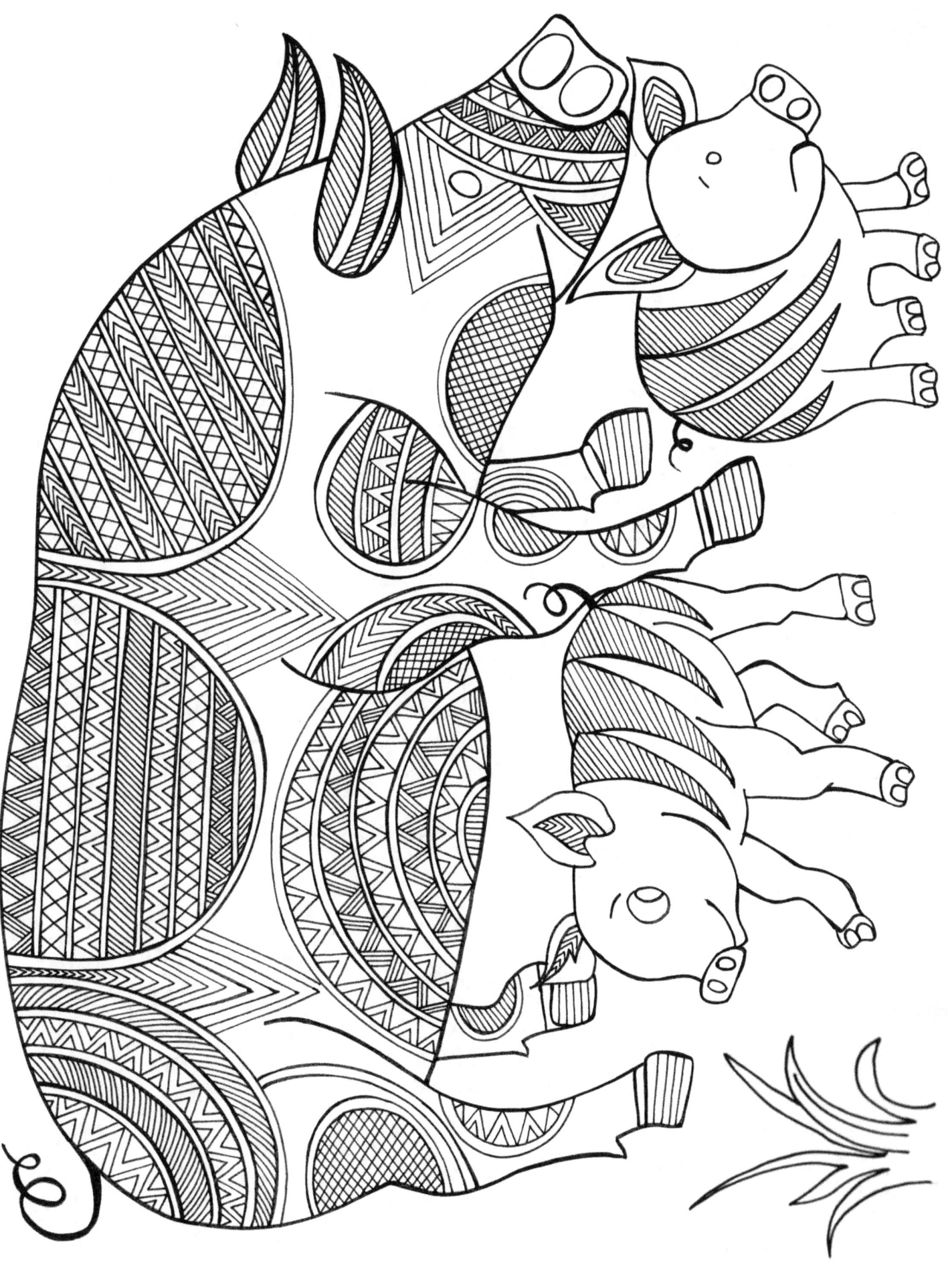

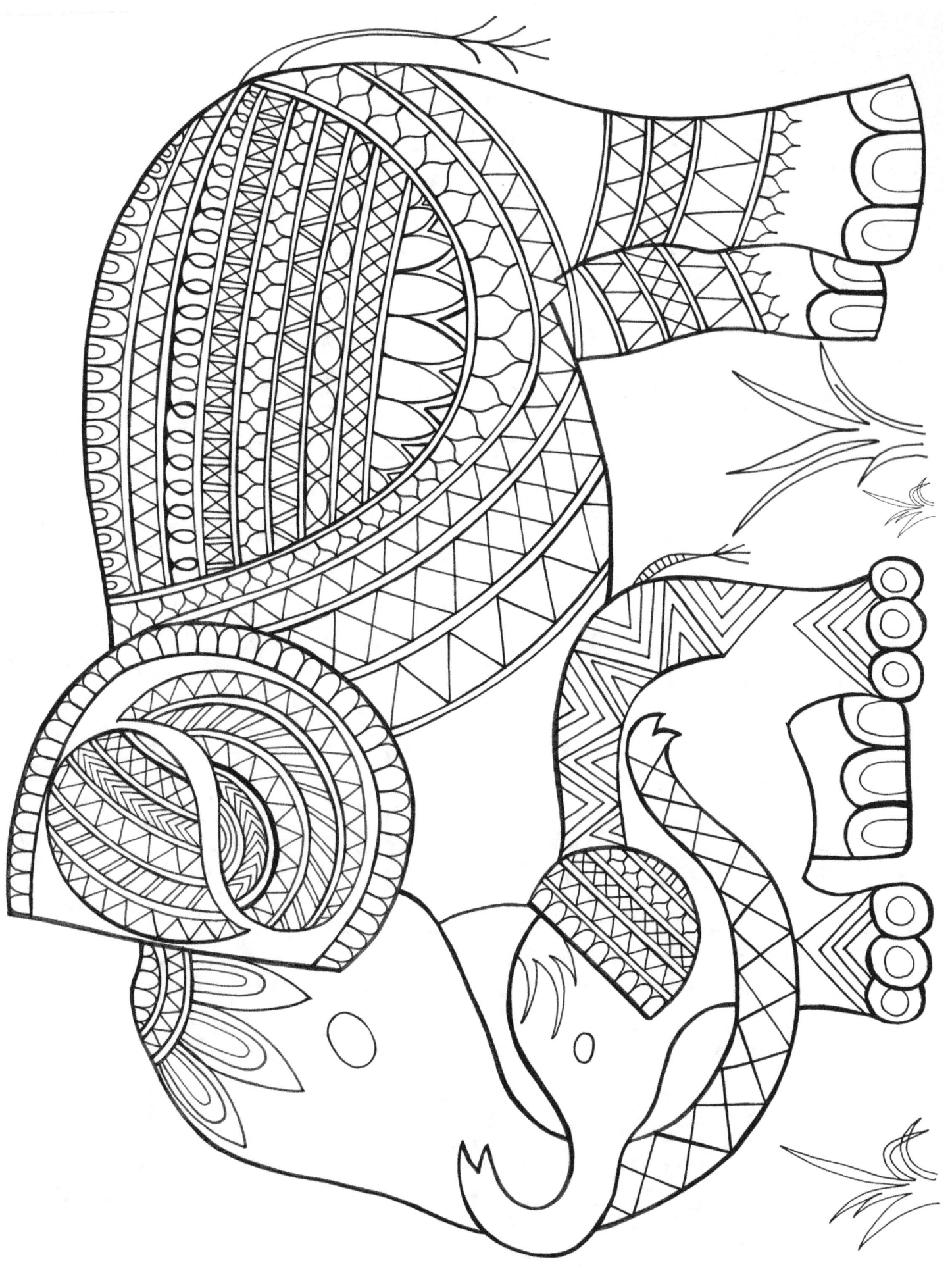

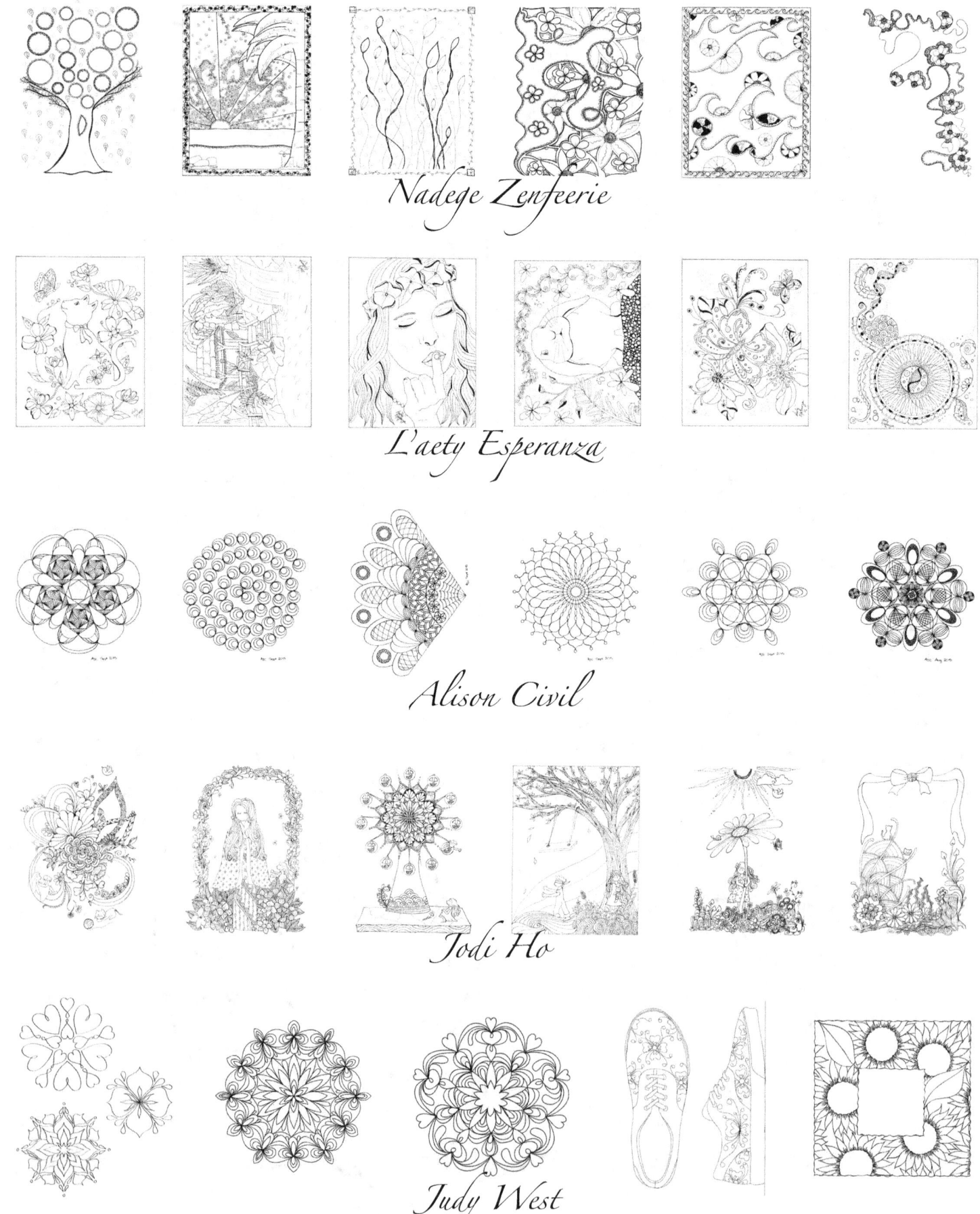

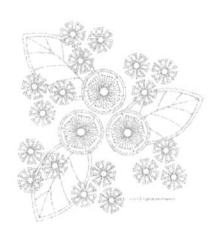 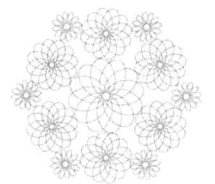 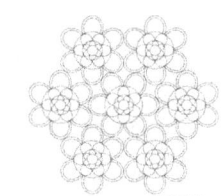 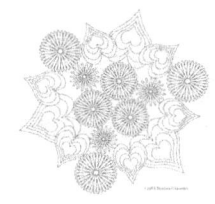 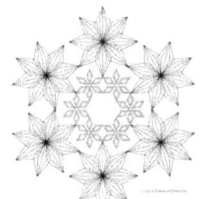 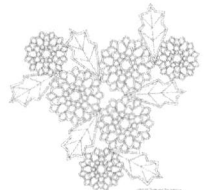

Tamara A. Cameron

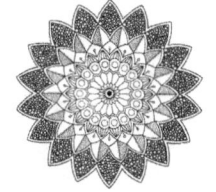 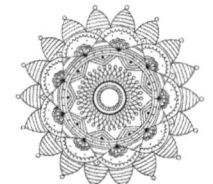 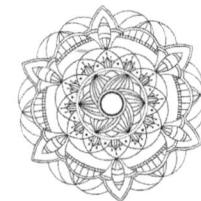 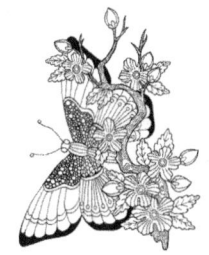 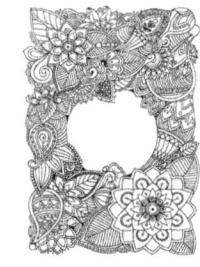

Heba Seada

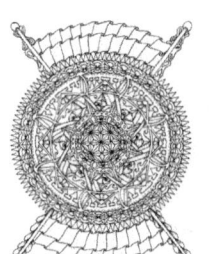 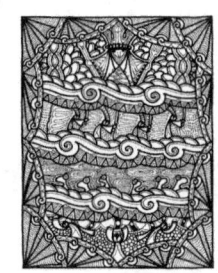 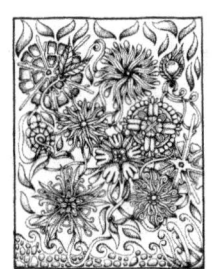 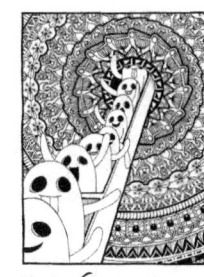 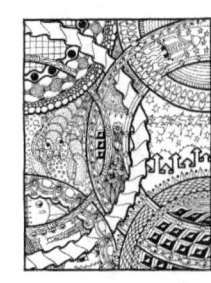 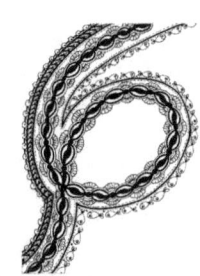

Pica Wu

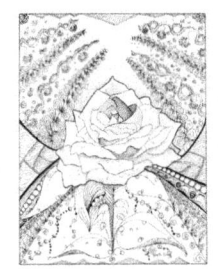 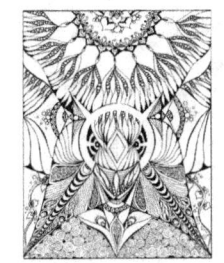 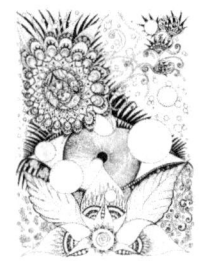 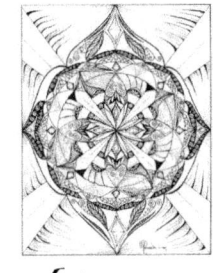 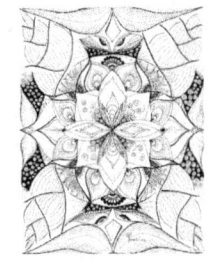 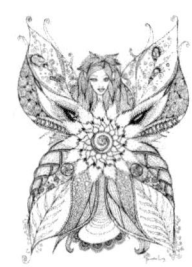

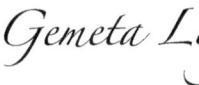

Gemeta Ling

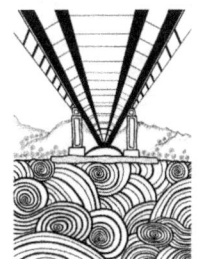 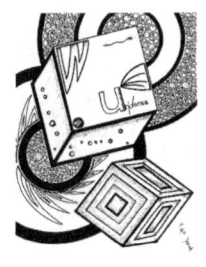 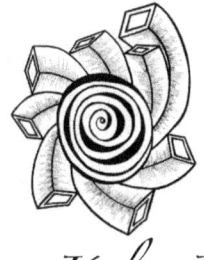 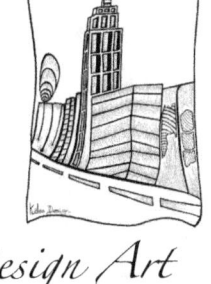 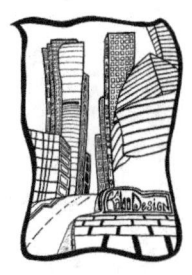 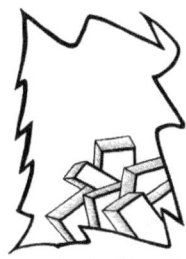

Kaloo Design Art

Test your colors here on the samples from
"My Pocket Coloring Companion"
&
"My Coloring Companion"

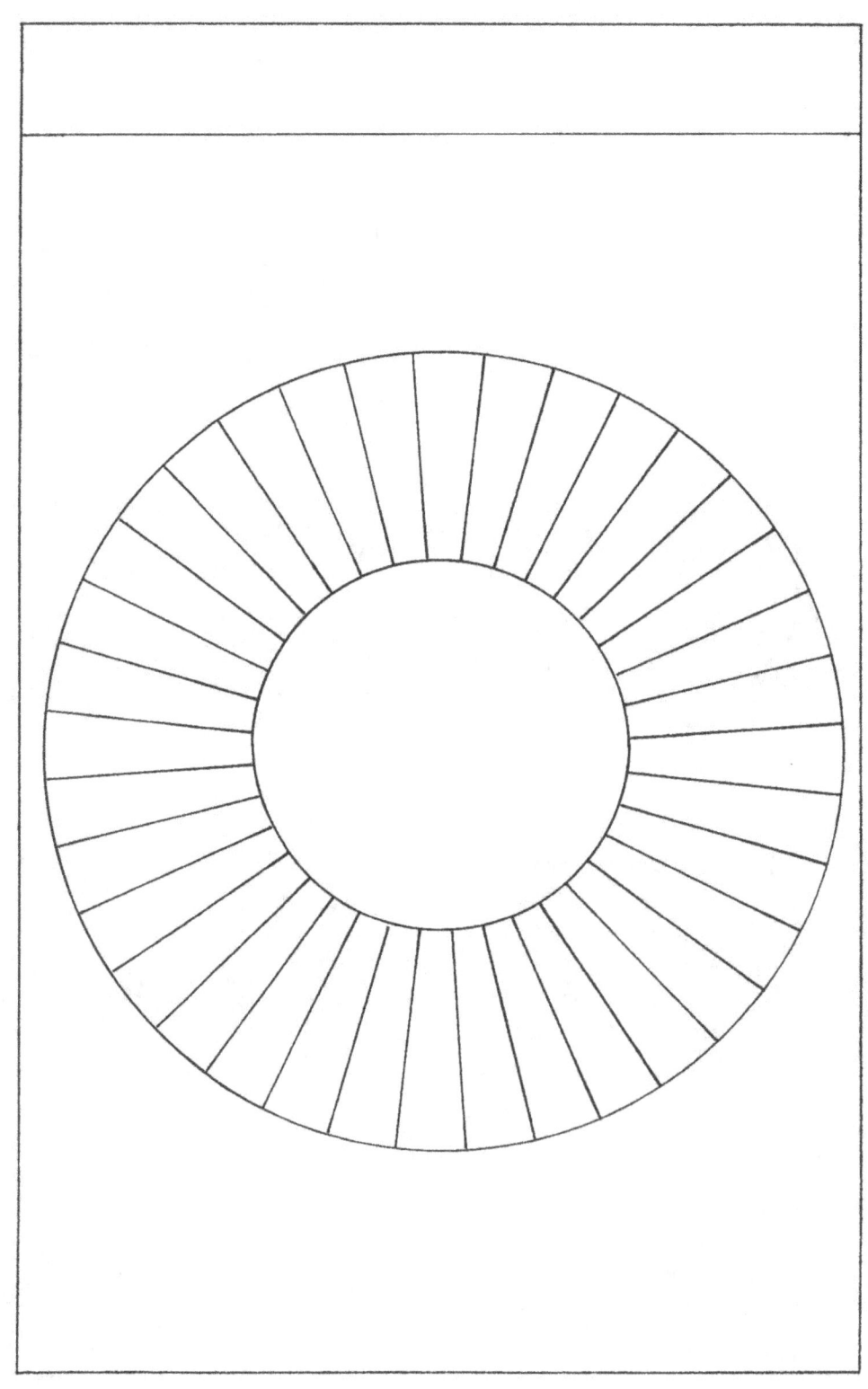

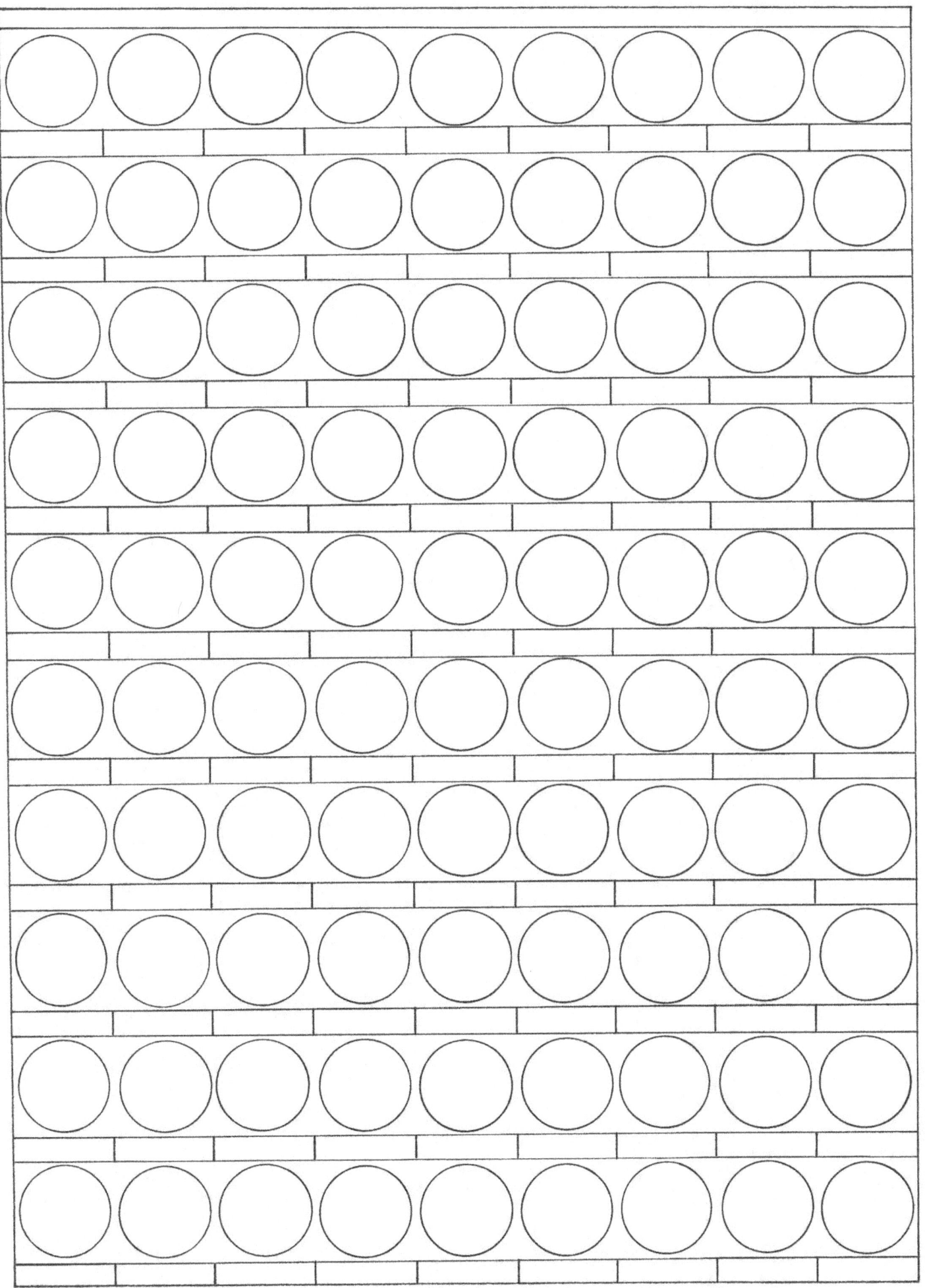

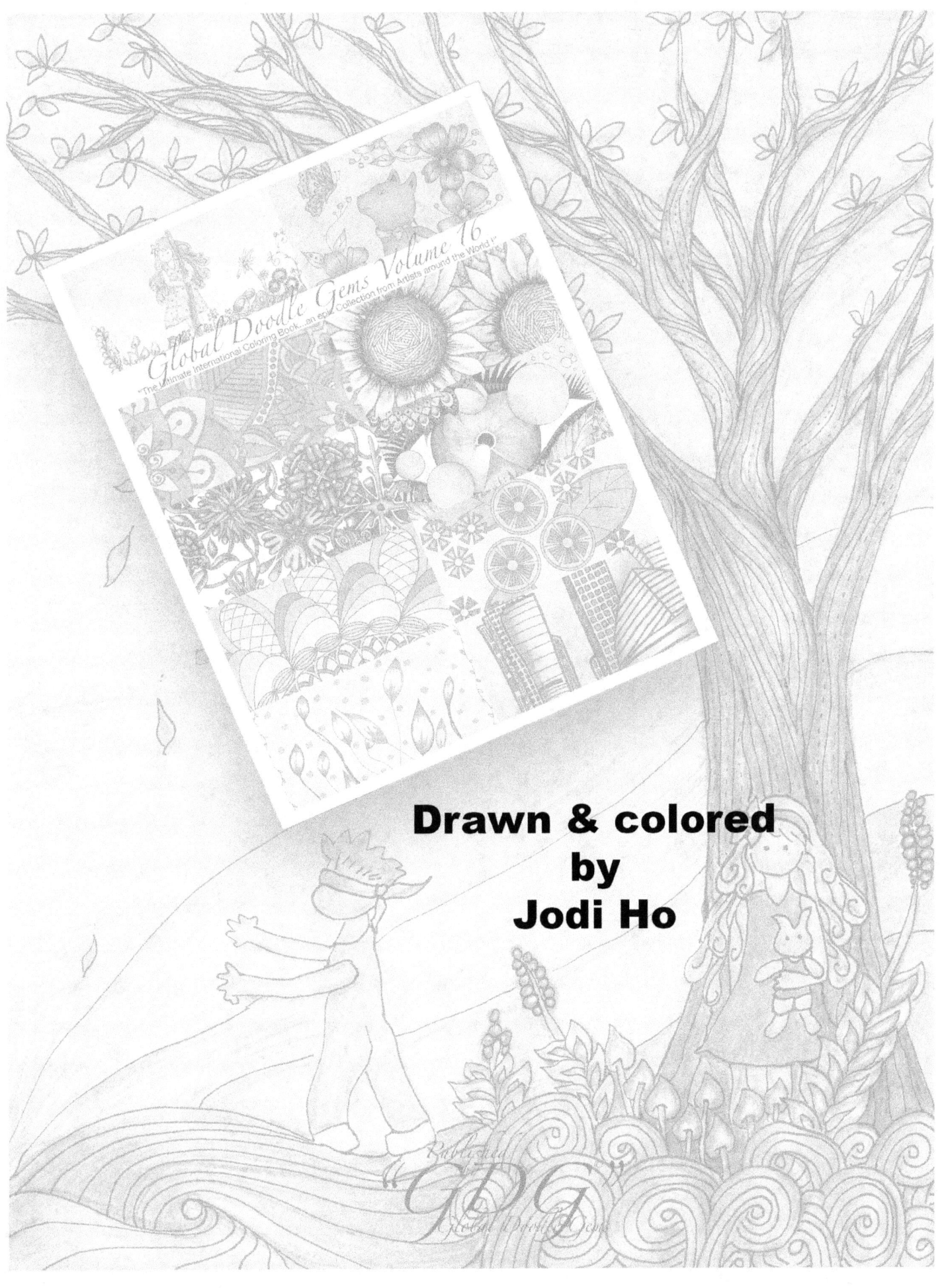

Drawn & colored by Jodi Ho